MW00710577

Kathy's Journey: Roots & Wings

Eugene Flynn

An E. Flynn Seminars Book

Kildeer, IL

Mari Beth,
Peace in Christ,
Gene Fly

E. Flynn Seminars
PO Box 156
Lake Zurich, IL 60047-0156

ISBN: 0-9729514-0-7

E. Flynn Seminars
www.eflynnseminars.com

This book is dedicated to the memory
of Katherine Lane Flynn and to the
St. Francis de Sales faith community

Kathy's Journey: Roots & Wings

Contents

ACKNOWLEDGEMENTS

I received help from many special people as I prepared this book.

To name just a few, Kathy's aunt Victorine Hays gave key insight on the Fitzmaurice Family; Kathy's sister Pat Janowiak and cousin Jacqueline Lane Niesen added information about the Lane families; and Jack Hays shared key baseball and Harry Lane stories.

Kathy's lifelong friends Martha Fowler Campbell, Judy Scornavacco Hoffman and Carol Goggin Dempsey filled in missing pieces of Kathy's high school and college days. Loyola ISP "Study Buddy" Jackie Froehlich also shared stories of Kathy Master Degree studies.

My aunt, Margaret Lyons RSM shared stories, records, and pictures of my Lyons heritage.

Lastly, Helen Weinfurter RSM did the final proofreading and saved me from the many errors that even spellcheckers could not catch.

Kathy's Journey: Roots & Wings

Family Members

Grandparents to Kathy and Eugene Flynn

John Lane married Katherine Brennan
Children: Harry, John, Willis, and Ellen

Patrick Fitzmaurice married Mary Higgins
Children: Marie, Loretta, Margurite, Helen, Catherine,
Tom and Victorine

Roger Lyons married Mary Sullivan
Children: Mary, Alice, Eugene, Margaret, and Roger

James Flynn married Kate Lavin
Children: Agnes, James, Irene, Frank, Catherine, Fran,
Nell, and Bernadette.

Parents (Lane, Hays & Flynn)

Harry Lane married Catherine Fitzmaurice
Children: Patricia, Judith, and Katherine (Kathy)

John Lane married Mildred Klunk
Children: Jacqueline and Barbara

John Hays married Victorine Fitzmaurice
Child: John

Frank Flynn married Mary Lyons
Children: Ellen, James, Laurette, Eugene and Margaret

ix

Kathy's Journey: Roots & Wings

Introduction

*"In the journey of life, the journey we
begin is not always the journey we end."*
(Lesson from J.R.R. Tolkien's *The Hobbit*)

Kathy Lane Flynn, my wife of 30 years, died suddenly of a heart attack in January 2002. This book is the story of the people that touched her life and how she touched the lives of others. And because her life journey was intertwined with those around her and those that preceded her, it includes the stories of many different people. The stories span four generations, beginning with grandparents born in the 1880's and 1890's.

And while family and friends were key factors in Kathy's life, most of these people were part of a dynamic city during 20th Century America. This too touched her life.

I started this writing effort shortly after coming back from a golf trip with college friends Ken Cunniff and Mike Mann. We golfed in the afternoons, which gave us mornings and evenings to relax and enjoy the beautiful scenery in Palm Springs, California. One morning Mike and I spent two hours talking about our families and the meaning of life; at one point he exclaimed: "You Irish, you love to tell stories!"

Kathy also loved to share stories. When I completed the first manuscript draft I gave a copy to our friend and pastor, Rev. Ron Gollatz. When he asked how long did it take to write it, I could truthfully reply: "Thirty years to collect the stories and ten days to record them."

1

Story Telling

Stories are a wonderful way for sharing ideas and values. I think this is true in part because good stories can give us something to think about, regardless of our age. As our lives change, that same story can take on new meaning and help us see new options in life.

Novels, TV and movies are great ways to see and hear stories. However, there are many great stories right within our own families that are well worth sharing.

Children and teens can benefit from learning how grandparents, parents, aunts and uncles faced joys and sorrows during their passage to adulthood. After all, children see older family members as fully-grown and find it hard see any connection with what they are going though as teenagers.

Family stories can bridge part of the gap between generations by showing that the journey in life often includes mistakes and confusion, as well as a helping hand along the way. All this was certainly true in Kathy's journey.

Lessons from Stories

The last chapter of this book gives a summary of some lessons Kathy learned along her journey. Those of you that read the intervening chapters can draw your own conclusions.

Chapter 1:

Kathy Remembered

We buried Kathy at All Saints Cemetery on Thursday, January 16th, 2002. She had died of a massive heart attack the previous Sunday night. While Kathy had many illnesses in her life, the heart attack was sudden and unexpected.

Over 800 people came to the wake the night before and 700 came to the funeral mass. Both were held at St. Francis de Sales Catholic Church[1], where Kathy served as Pastoral Associate.

While some came as family members or friends, the vast majority were people Kathy ministered to over the previous 10 years. Some were teens or young adults that Kathy worked with when they were in grammar or high school. Others were catechists and leaders from Religious Education. Still others were people she had worked with to plan a wedding or apply for a marriage annulment. Kathy had clearly touched many lives.

Our friend and pastor, Fr. Ron Gollatz, gave the homily and spoke of the many times that Kathy had been willing to venture from a safe situation into new territory. Kathy had even asked Ron to dance at a turnabout dance at the Catholic grammar school they both attended. Kathy was in seventh grade at the time and Ron was in 8th grade.

Ron knew of Kathy and her family because both families lived in the same tight-knit community of Our Lady Help of Christians on Chicago's west side.

---

[1] Catholic Archdiocese of Chicago

Extended Families

The parish family came to comfort Kathy's family, and we came to comfort the people of Saint Francis; they were also part of Kathy's family. Kathy was a Lane daughter by birth, and the Lane brothers, her father and uncle, had a history of finding large extended families.

Photo Albums

In the weeks following the funeral I was back at work and busy with insurance forms and writing thank-you cards. I also packed Kathy's clothing to give to different people and charities. Kathy took how she dressed very seriously, and worked to look professional even as her weight dropped over the last two years.

I also began to scan photos from the many different photo albums around the house; our basement seemed to be the resting place for generations of albums. I eventually burned a CD contained 300 Photo sorted into 12 different files. Files included: Kathy's parents, Kathy's grand-parents, Kathy's childhood, Gene & Kathy, young David Flynn, Florida vacations, my parents, Msgr. Eugene Lyons, and my grand-parents. I even had a file with ten pictures of Flynn dogs.

The photographs cover a span of 75 years. They show Irish families on the west side of Chicago between the world wars as they achieved some economic security and saw renewed hardship during the great depression. They also show families on many happy occasions like newborn babies, first communions, weddings, and even ordinations to the priesthood.

I had already started to distribute copies of CD to a number of family members within both the Flynn family and the Lane family.

But I felt something was missing. A picture of Kathy's grandparents, parents or uncle John does not convey the impact they had on her life.

This document is an attempt to tell the story of how Kathy came to be a Pastoral Associate able to touch so many lives and how the journey she ended was not the journey she started.

Our Lives and Roots are Intertwined

Several months after Kathy died, I learned a 2nd cousin of Kathy's was having a hard time dealing with her death. I planned to visit Kelly and bring her and her 5-year-old daughter a small gift from Kathy's jewelry collection. While rummaging around Kathy's jewelry drawer, I found 20 cards showing a green tree and the words: "In the tree of life, our Roots are Forever Intertwined[2]. The poem on the back speaks to this message.

Kelly received a set of earrings, an Irish sweater and the "Our Roots are intertwined" card. Her daughter, Molly, received a small music box and a silly looking Reindeer pin that Kathy liked to wear at Christmas time.

Kelly told me that she felt bad that she never told Kathy how much Kathy meant to her. That as a teenager she felt so welcomed at our house and hoped that

---

[2] Forest of Peace Publishing – 1-800-659-3227 <or> www.forestofpeace.com

someday she could have a marriage like Kathy's. I assured her that Kathy knew of her feelings because they were present in the large green teddy bear that Kelly made for us and in the playful spirit that she and our son called each other "Ugly baby."

Chapter 2:

Kathy & Gene Meet

I met Kathy Lane in November 1969 at a post-Thanksgiving party hosted by Jay Krakora and his cousin Lynn Muldoon. Kathy and Jay were friends since grammar school and I was there with Jay's cousin Ray Williams.

I had left the Catholic seminary the previous August and was working on a Masters Degree in Sociology at Northern Illinois University in DeKalb, Illinois. We talked at the party and found we had a lot of common interests.

I called Kathy from school the following week and asked her out on a date. We went to see the Arthur Miller play *All of My Children* followed by dinner at a German restaurant. The evening should have been a bust because the play was pretty depressing and Kathy later told me she didn't like German food. However something must have sparked her interest because Kathy agreed to a second date to attend Christmas midnight Mass a few weeks later.

Different Cloth

I was certainly cut from a different cloth than the guys Kathy had dated and hung out with over the previous 6-7 years. I was dressed in black pants and a coat that had never been in style. More importantly, I was very new to dating and rough on social skills. Once when calling for a date, I told Kathy that "dating someone in Chicago was not part of my current plan, but I wanted to date her anyway" (lucky Kathy).

Kathy, on the other hand, had been dating throughout high school and college. The young men she dated took their relationship much more seriously than she did. She declined her first offer of marriage in high school. When Kathy and I met, she had recently ended a 3-year relationship and was not looking to become serous with anyone for a while.

Throughout the winter and spring of 1970, I came back from DeKalb every weekend to spend time with Kathy. We saw each other on most Saturday nights and usually on Sunday as well, often going to parties or spending time with her friends. Most nights ended with an hour together in the front room of the apartment Kathy shared with her mother.

In the summer of 1970 Kathy and I continued to spend most weekends together, including a trip to the Flynn summer home on Lake Delavan, Wisconsin.

This trip gave Kathy a chance to meet the Flynn family for the first time. Kathy was impressed that grandmother Lyons did reprimand her son Monsignor Lyons and grandson Gene Flynn for being slow at helping the guests. Kathy thought Mary helped ground both son and grandson.

To Pittsburgh and Back

By August I had finished my Masters work and was preparing to enter the Ph.D. program at the University of Pittsburgh. Before leaving I asked Kathy to marry me. She said she was not ready to make a decision as serious as that. I think she had used the same line several times before.

I went off to the University of Pittsburgh and would often call Kathy. However, it was clear that keeping an active relationship over the phone was not very practical. By November, I decided I didn't need a Ph.D. In mid-December I was back in Chicago and had lined up a job at the Illinois Department of Labor. On New Year's Eve I asked Kathy for a second time to be my wife; this time she accepted.

She would later joke that she said "yes" only because of drinking too much Cold Duck at a party earlier that night. Do they still make Cold Duck?

Spark of Interest

The 'spark of interest' on Kathy's part after our first few dates changed my life. She looked beyond my social miscues and saw a kindred spirit.

I attribute it in large part to the core values that she gained from her parents, Harry and Catherine Lane.

Chapter 3:

Harry Lane's Story

Harry Lane was born in 1906, the second of five children for John and Katherine Lane. His father was a Railroad conductor for the Chicago & Northwestern RR and mother was a graduate[3] of a Woman's college in Iowa. At the time, a conductor was one of the best paying job among the Irish on the west side.

However, the good life that young Harry enjoyed fell apart before he was twelve. His mother and two siblings died from heart conditions or influenza[4] within a twelve-month period, leaving just the father, Harry, and John, age ten.

Within the year the boy's father married Katherine's sister, Belle. She was a kind woman and tried to make a good home for her husband and two stepchildren.

Harry would talk to "Aunt Belle" and try to be friendly. John had lots of anger over the death of his mother and would barely say hello to his stepmother.

Off to Archbishop Mundelein's Prep School

Harry and John lost their close family, but they did not lose connection to the Irish Catholic community. At age 13 Harry enrolled at Quigley Preparatory Seminary

---

[3] In the late 1800's graduating from college did not necessarily mean finishing 16 years of schooling. Many colleges covered what is currently covered in the last two years of high school and the first year of college.

[4] The 1918 Influenza outbreak was a worldwide health crisis that killed 20 million people, more than all of World War I. In the US 500,000 people died, with approximately 10,000 of the deaths in Chicago. It is almost impossible for us in the 21st century to contemplate this level of human suffering.

in 1919. His daughter Pat thinks that Harry was fulfilling his mother's deathbed wish.

I am also sure the sisters at Saint Matthew Parish thought that Harry was a bright and outgoing boy who would make a fine priest.

The program must have been OK with Harry because he spent nearly eleven years in the Archdiocese of Chicago Seminary system.

Quigley was a high school seminary just opened by Archbishop George Mundelein. Archbishop Mundelein was a native of New York City and most recently Auxiliary Bishop of Brooklyn. One of his first moves when installed in early 1916 was to begin planning a high school seminary modeled after Cathedral Preparatory Seminary in New York City. Chicago's version opened in 1918 and was located three blocks from Holy Name Cathedral.

Archbishop Mundelein was sent to Chicago to bring the Archdiocese up to the "major league" ranks along with Boston, New York and Philadelphia. Chicago had grown from 1.1 million people in 1890 to 2.2 million in 1910. It had a huge immigrant Catholic population and needed a real leader to push and pull all the disorganized pieces together.

By the time he was created Cardinal Priest on March 24, 1924, George Mundelein was well on his way to reshaping the Catholic Church in Chicago and to a lesser extent, the Lane and Lyons families.

Life at Quigley

Harry Lane entered Quigley Preparatory Seminary in 1918, nine years ahead of Gene Lyons and 40+ years ahead of Jim Flynn and Gene Flynn. Despite the span of years, we all received basically the same education that emphasized Latin, Greek, English Literature, English Composition, Religion, History, Math, and a <u>little</u> science. The teachers were largely Catholic priests chosen for leadership ability and academic skills.

One surviving photo shows Harry and 39 of his classmates in the Quigley courtyard. Harry is seated on the pavement, along with Lyons, McGovern, Lyons, and O'Gorman. All are wearing suits and look quite serious. Harry's nickname was "shorty"; in later years he would be called "big Red."

While students lived at home, Quigley was intended to be a relatively closed society where students socialized with each other and avoided non-Quigley students, especially girls. Using the French seminary model of holding classes on Saturday with Thursdays off also encouraged friendships based on Quigley boundaries.

We have five surviving books from Harry's Quigley days. Each has his name and address (2936 Fulton Street). Besides Shakespeare's *Macbeth* and *Julius Ceasar*, the books include:

- The Art of Oratorical Composition by Charles Coppens, S.J. © 1885 by The Catholic Publication Society, NYC.

- A Practical Introduction to English Rhetoric by Charles Coppens, S.J. © 1886 by The Catholic Publication Society, NYC.
- Outlines of Rhetoric by John Genung, © 1883. Ginn & Company, Boston.

Between his Irish wit and this much rhetoric, is it any wonder that Harry was so well spoken.

The Quigley yearbook for 1924 gives the following information about Harry:

Harry Thomas Lane
St. Matthew Parish
"Shorty"
Catechist, 1921-1922
Gregorian choir, 1923-1924
Chaplain in play *Sir Thomas More*

No mention is made of athletic accomplishments.

John Lane

Meanwhile, John Lane spent three years at Saint Patrick High School, graduating in June 1924. St. Patrick prepared its students for clerical jobs in the Chicago business world; typing, bookkeeping, and writing skills were stressed.

The school also had a major strength in finding jobs for its students. The Best of the typing students went to the Chicago Police Department. John was among this group and began working for the CPD as a Stenographer/Typist upon his graduation in 1925. He would later become a police officer when he reached the minimum required age.

Both of the Lane boys received excellent high school educations.

In the 1920s most first and second generation Irish did not finish high school and very few went to college. Sixteen-year-old girls could start at Illinois Bell or Sears Roebuck and get any training they needed on the job. Likewise, boys could begin working on the railroad or at factories that lined the near west and near north side.

Major Seminary

In 1924, Harry Lane entered Saint Mary of the Lake Seminary in Mechanics Grove, Illinois. He was to spend three years in the Philosophy undergraduate program before beginning four years in the Theology wing of the campus.

This 1,100-acre campus, which opened in 1922, marked a key achievement for Archbishop George Mundelein. He had started the effort in 1920 with a $500,000 donation by lumber merchant Edward Hines. The piers and walkways at the head of the Saint Mary's Lake were named in honor of Hines' son who died in France during World War I.

Mundelein spared no expense to create a seminary system that he hoped would attract students from many dioceses and religious orders. Joseph McCarthy, a young Catholic architect, was commissioned to design the entire campus in an early American, neo-classical style to symbolize the "American commitment" of the Catholic Church. The cardinal's residence on campus was a reproduction of George Washington's Mount Vernon home.

Saint Mary of the Lake soon became one of the largest major seminaries in the US. In 1926 the Archdiocese of Chicago hosted the International Eucharistic Congress, which drew hundreds of thousands of people to large events at Chicago's Soldier Field and the major seminary in the newly renamed town of Mundelein, Illinois.

We are not sure if Harry Lane ever met personally with Bishop and later Cardinal Mundelein; but we can be sure that he heard Mundelein preach often when the Cardinal stayed at the "Cardinal's residence." Then and later the Cardinal was a big believer in "American Values," in social justice, and in Catholic doctrine.

The Major Seminary[5]

Harry Lane's life at Saint Mary's was very structured. The day began at 5.35 AM with a knock on the door of each student's private room. The seminarian assigned wake-up duties would call out in a loud voice: "Benedicamus Domino (Let us praise the lord)"; each waking seminarian was to reply "Deo Gratias (Thanks be to God)." Weekdays included three hours of spiritual exercises, four classes and 4-5 hours of study. Core classes in Philosophy and Theology were conducted in Latin by Jesuit professors in the scholastic methods of St. Thomas Aquinas. Reading newspapers, magazines, and novels was not permitted, nor were radios allowed.

---

[5] Architecture and daily schedule from "Saint Mary of the Lake Seminary, 75 years: a History" by Dr. Edward Kantowicz. *Saint Mary of the Lake Bridge*, Spring 1997.

The major seminary was planned as a self-contained environment. Students left the grounds only for two weeks in late January and for assigned summer duties. Family members were allowed to visit one Sunday afternoon a month. Students that violated the many rules were quickly ordered to leave.

By the way, these rules remained largely in effect through my brother Jim's attendance in the 1960s. When I arrived in 1967 for the final two years of college, students had almost total freedom to come and go, as they liked. Even attending mass and classes was optional.

Harry Lane attended Saint Mary of the Lake for nearly six years. He was about 15 months away from ordination when he left Saint Mary of the Lake in late 1931. We don't know what prompted his leaving, but we do know that Harry stayed very close to his classmates that were ordained in 1933 and that he loved to discuss Thomas Aquinas, Augustine and social justice around the dinner table.

Harry and the Fitzmaurice Family

While Harry lost his own close family life when his mother and three siblings died in 1918, he adopted the Fitzmaurice family sometime during high school. Patrick and Mary Fitzmaurice lived in the same Kedzie Avenue neighborhood. The six girls and one son included: Marie, Loretta, Margurite, Helen, Catherine, Tom and Victorine as the youngest. Harry was a couple years older than Catherine, his future wife. One surviving photo shows six Fitzmaurice children sitting on a front step.

Patrick Fitzmaurice had made good money at Griffin Wheel iron-works, firm that produced iron wheels for railroad cars. His job as a molder required him to prepare the wheel mold and monitor the pouring of the molten steel. In the 1920's Foundry men typically worked 12-hour shifts, rotating from days to nights every month.

However, by the mid-1920's Pat's work life was largely over. Rheumatoid Arthritis and many burns had taken their toll.

Any accident payments or insurance ended very shortly. Because this was before Social Security or general disability insurance, the family lost essentially all sources of income. While the local parish and neighbors helped, survival of the family largely depended on the daughters going to work.

Fitzmaurice Daughters

The girls did pitch in and kept the family afloat. Marie, Margurite and Helen worked for Sears Roebuck from age 16 or 17. Marie eventually rose to Director of Accounting, one of the highest-ranking women employees in the 1950s. One surviving photo shows Marie at her seated desk. Margurite became an executive secretary and left Sears quite wealthy due to employee profit sharing, a concept started at Sears.

With skill and a very firm hand, Mary Fitzmaurice held the family together and appearances up. They even had room in their heart to welcome high school student Harry Lane into their fold. Or perhaps he just showed up; the Irish were reluctant to ask anyone to leave.

The Fitzmaurice family got by with very little money in part because they lived in an area of Chicago where people had experience in poverty, even if most of them were doing well in the boom period of the 1920s. Rents were low; no one needed a car and food was stretched to make do.

Victorine Fitzmaurice Hays remembers that her mother had two firm rules: 1) Unless you were working, you had to be at the family dinner each evening, and 2) Once you gave a piece of clothing to a sister, you couldn't ask for it back. Mary was a very wise woman.

When the depression hit with full force in 1930, many neighbors joined the Fitzmaurice family at or near poverty levels. However, the Fitzmaurice daughters did not feel overly poor and were enjoying life as teens and young adults. Vic certainly remembers it that way. And Catherine Fitzmaurice certainly had a great sense of humor her entire life. It was one of her many gifts to daughter Kathy.

Mundelein College Opens

The year 1929 marked the start of the great depression and the opening of a new Catholic women's college in Chicago. As a 5th generation American educated in Rome, George Cardinal Mundelein wanted to promote a Chicago Catholic Church that was 100% American[6] and 100% devoted to the doctrines of the

---

[6] Cardinal Mundelein was a friend of Frank D. Roosevelt and hosted the president in October 1937. In May of the same year, Cardinal Mundelein verbally lashed out against Hitler for the fears and slavery that were being practiced by the Nazi party. His words were treated as "hot news"; for example, *The Houston*

Catholic. He also wanted to keep Catholic students out of what he considered anti-Catholic Northwestern University and The University of Chicago.

The new women's college was to be run by the Sisters of Charity of the Blessed Virgin Mary (BVM) and named Mundelein College in honor the Cardinal. In future years, Kathy Lane and her sister Pat would attend Mundelein College.

Even apart from the cardinal's feelings about non-Catholic schools, Chicago desperately needed more college capacity. The city had grown to 3.4 million people by 1930 and was being served by a handful of medium-size colleges[7]. It was only after World War II that Roosevelt University, the University of Illinois at Chicago Circle, and Governor's State University came into existence.

Harry Courts Catherine

When Harry left the seminary in 1931, Catherine Fitzmaurice was already working for Illinois Bell as a switchboard operator. She worked a split shift with hours in the morning and hours in the evening.

Press ran a May 20, 1937 headline: "Nazi Protest U.S. Cardinal's Hitler Attack." Sadly, Cardinal Mundelein was one of only a handful of Catholic Church leaders in the US or Europe that spoke publicly against Nazi Germany. George Cardinal Mundelein died at the outset of World War II on October 2, 1939.

[7] For example, Loyola University Chicago had over 3,000 new gradutes in 2002, but averaged only 250 new graduates/year during the last three years of the 1920's. (Source: Loyola University Chicago)

Mary Fitzmaurice encouraged her daughters to delay marriage while they continued to support the family. After all, they provided the only income and Vic and Tom were still too young to work.

The family did make an exception for Catherine to marry Harry when she was only 24. Harry was 27.

Harry and Catherine married in 1933. The wedding reception was held in the back yard of the Fitzmaurice apartment. The Kodak photos show the six Fitzmaurice girls with aunt Helen, and husband, from California. Other photos show the wedding party including John Lane and "Shorty" Shanahan, a friend from Quigley days.

Extended Families

Many young men might hesitate to marry into such a close-knit family with many demands on your presence and support. Some might even suggest that relocation to California might be in order. Harry had no such fears. He had won the love of his life and the extended family of his dreams.

Meanwhile John Lane had joined the Chicago Police Department. He started as a Police Stenographer on his graduation and later became a Police Officer in one of the districts. While only holding the rank of Sergeant, John eventually became Administrative Assistant to two police commissioners.

John would eventually move to the Chicago Board of Health at the request of Mayor Richard J. Daley, but the Chicago Police Department was always his first love.

Chapter 4:

Harry and Catherine Lane

Harry began work selling advertising in the sales department of the Chicago Tribune. His friends told the story that Harry and five other salesmen (this was before they had sales women at the Tribune) were laid off during a depression cut back. Harry however, kept coming to work and after a while the manager finally gave up and kept him on the payroll. Harry was well liked and could tell great stories.

Harry and Catherine had daughter Patricia in 1935 and daughter Judith in 1937. Harry did not go off to fight in WWII. However, his growing responsibilities at the Tribune and within the Fitzmaurice family kept him very busy. Harry enjoyed his financial success and enjoyed partying with his coworkers, his neighborhood friends, and his seminary classmates that were ordained in 1933.

Harry and Catherine were living a good life. In 1946 they purchased a three-story apartment building in partnership with Catherine's sister, Marie Fitzmaurice. Their new address was 1109 North LeClaire Avenue. While they had previously rented in the same neighborhood, it was clear that the Lanes were taking roots in Our Lady Help of Christian (HOC) parish.

Children around the house

The Lane apartment and a rented summer home on Lake Geneva became the new hub for the Lane/Fitzmaurice families. Kathy's cousin Jacqueline Lane remembers running up and down the stairs, jumping on beds and creating havoc with Pat and Judy while Harry and Catherine encouraged the fun. Harry loved to take John's daughters to see the White Sox Baseball, knowing that John was a Chicago Cub fan.

While Harry and Catherine had few rules for the children, there were some important ones, including:

- Every child got to play and none was excluded.
- Children did their own homework and projects
- The daughters could watch TV, but only in the unfinished basement (it never got much use).

Kathy Lane Arrives

In 1947 Catherine was pregnant again after several miscarriages. The baby came two months early on March 18, 1947. Survival of mother and child was at great risk for the first 24 hours. The baby was named Katherine and came home a week later. Catherine stayed an extra three weeks at old St. Joseph's Hospital in Chicago. A neighborhood woman came in to care for the now three Lane girls; it was rumored that Harry never changed a diaper in his life.

Catherine and Kathy were under the care of young Dr. Frank Murphy, recently released from the US Army Medical Service. Frank Murphy was to become a friend of Harry Lane and would care for Kathy and Catherine Lane for the next 35 years.

Kathy Lane had entered a financially successful family. They had a large and well-furnished apartment and a housekeeper that came twice a week.[8]

Harry had many chances to move the family to upscale River Forest or even to Minnesota as a VP for a big advertising company. After much discussion, Harry and Catherine stayed in place. Harry could own a luxury automobile, winter in Miami Beach and summer on Lake Geneva. However, with Catherine's strong encouragement, he stayed close to his west side roots and his extended family.

Harry left the Tribune on good terms and started his own business selling advertising space in magazines. His main customers were big-three auto firms in Detroit. With his personality, skills and many contacts, Harry was very successful in his own business.

Dinner Topics

Harry Lane was a liberal Democrat and loved to talk to the Lane daughters and their friends about politics, theology, and social issues. He challenged them to realize that racial prejudice was a real issue. He might ask:

- Is it fair that your favorite department store doesn't hire Negro sales-clerks?

---

[8] The author Fr. Andrew Greeley grew up in Saint Angela Parish, one parish west of Our Lady Help of Christians. A number of his books, including *Summer At the Lake* (Fore Book, NY, NY © 1997) portray upwardly mobile Irish families that lived near Oak Park and summered at Lake Geneva, Wisconsin.

- Should Blacks be allowed to purchase homes in Oak Park?

I don't think he expected the girls to boycott the department store, but he might have hoped to deflate a common belief that prejudice and discrimination were problems in Southern states and not a real issue in Chicago.

Harry did not live to see Martin Luther King lead 1967 marches in Chicago for open housing or for Chicago to be branded "most segregated city in America." Harry might have said: "I told you so."

Chapter 5

Our Lady Help of Christians

It is probably difficult for anyone born after 1970 to appreciate the urban parish experience of the 1940's and 1950's. At that time, Catholics were often a majority of the local population and their parish was the center for social interaction. People could go downtown for social and cultural events, but locally, the Catholic parish was typically the only game in town[9].

And while there were some non-Catholics around and even some public school, they were not very relevant to the Catholic parishioners. Essentially all Catholic parents sent their children to the parish school and most maintained a parish-centered social-life.

Catholics were forbidden to join the YMCA, but it really was not a big issue because the parish schools had lots of activities, teens could compete in the citywide Catholic Youth Organization (CYO) or at their Catholic high school, and the Chicago Park District had a field house in most neighborhoods. And if the Catholic parishes were largely composed of one or maybe two ethnic groups, no one seemed to mind.[10]

---

[9] My hunch is that remote suburban communities like Lake Zurich and Barrington had more diverse social options in the 1940's and 1950's. Catholics were often a much lower percentage of the population, many Catholic went to public schools, and organizations like the Lions and VFW were alive and active in the communities.

[10] Lest we get carried away with nostalgia, we should also recognize that while most 1950's parishes were no longer based on ethnic heritage, one or two ethnic groups were usually more prevalent at any

Each parish was pretty much a kingdom to itself, and the clear ruler was the pastor. Answering only the Cardinal, the pastor assigned all duties to the many associate pastors, had final authority at the school, and appointed laypeople to leadership positions as he saw fit.

Perhaps the local taverns were the only significant area of the community where the pastor did not have a controlling voice. He could speak against drinking, but the taverns had a license from city hall. However, they usually had to close at midnight on Saturday and could not reopen until Sunday afternoon.

During the 1950's and 1960's, Our Lady Help of Christians (HOC) was a thriving and tight-knit community with a largely Irish and Italian ethnic composition. Based on the memories of past residents and a great Centennial Celebration Memorial Book[11], we have a lot of details about parish life when Kathy and her sisters were growing up. Some of these details include:

- In 1948, Msgr. Richard S. Kelly began construction on a new School Addition. Upon completion, there were 1,310 students attending the school. 1960 saw

---

specific parish; and parishioners liked it that way. Polish or Lithuanian families might not find the warmest of welcomes in a largely Irish or Irish/Italian parish. As for blacks and Hispanics, there would be no welcome at all.

[11] 1901-2001: A Century of Christian Experience, HOC Centennial Book, 2001.

the addition of a new school building and ten additional classrooms (for a total capacity of 1,700 students).

- In 1951, over 2,500 families belonged to the parish. The vast majority lived within ½ mile of the Church[12] and walked to and from parish activities. The only available parking was on the street.

- HOC was a dynamic and well-supported parish under the leadership of Msgr. Richard S. Kelly. (Pastor from 1936 to 1968, he later died in 1972, at the age of 80). Eighteen BVM sisters lived in the convent and seven priests lived in the rectory.

- Ron Gollatz graduated from HOC grammar school in 1960. The vast majority of the 80 boy graduates went to Catholic High School, including eight that went to Quigley Preparatory Seminary.

- Msgr. Kelly personally handed out every semester report cards and gave a word of praise or encouragement to each student.

---

[12] Five other Catholic churches surrounded HOC. St. Peter Canisus was exactly one mile north, St. Angela Church was one mile West, St. Lucy Church was one mile southwest, St. Thomas was one mile south and Our Lady of Angels was 1.5 miles East. Most people living more than ½ mile from HOC would probably be outside HOC boundaries.

- HOC had a 9:00 AM Sunday mass for the school children. Each class sat as a group with the Sister seated behind her 60 students. During Lent, the children were also expected to attend an 8:00 AM daily mass, followed by milk and donuts in the school hall.

HOC School

The BVM[13] Sisters were the heart of school. A number of them shared HOC memories in the parish Centennial book, including:

Sr. Mary Bernadita Finnegan
(1944 – 1958, Grade 1)

My first year at HOC was a big one to me. There were 1600 children in the school, and I had 78 first

---

[13] Founded in 1833 in Philadelphia, the first five Sisters of Charity, BVM were young Irish immigrants. Led by Mary Frances Clarke and Rev. Terence Donaghoe. In 1843, the young community migrated to Dubuque, Iowa, at the invitation of Bishop Matthias Loras. The pioneer BVMs soon discovered the immense need for education, particularly for girls. They established a boarding school on the prairie near Dubuque, which later became Clarke College. In 1867, the BVM sisters began educational ministry in Chicago. (Source: www.bvmcong.org. BVM archives are housed at the BVM Center in Dubuque, Iowa.

graders. All the children assembled in front of the school. When the bell rang, all stood still. At the second bell, all moved into their respective lines and marched into school in perfect order.

One of my favorite memories occurred on the first day of school. A little boy was trying to find where he belonged. His older brother in guiding him to his teacher told him to look for the smiling Sister. The little boy ran right up to me.

Sr. Mary Ann Patrice Durr
(1937-54 Grade 1; 1962-66 Grade 2)

First Confession was never easy because of our large classes. One of my notorious "divileens" was, for good reason, standing right next to me. Just as he was about to enter the confessional, he looked up at me and solemnly asked: "This is serious business, isn't it?" I agreed.

Sr. Mary Ann Regina Dobek
(1938-45, Grade 4)

Our Lady Help of Christians, my first mission, offered me wonderful experiences for my future life as a teacher. Families were very cooperative. Msgr. Kelly was a model administrator who showed great love and concern for his people. His daily visit to St. Ann's Hospital was an inspiration to all who knew him. I love to recall the beautiful fresco of Mary above the main altar in the church. Our Lady portrayed the image of a caring mother to her children. She was indeed our Lady Help of Christians.

Sr. Mary Madonna Morin (Noel)
(1958-62, Grade 6)

After the fire at Our Lady of Angels School, the surviving students were divided into three groups, and occupied classrooms at the Hay, the Orr, or Help of Christians. Sr. Mary Madonna's responsibility was each afternoon to bring milk and cookies to the OLA children in HOC classrooms. When she got to Sr. Mary Virginetta's room, the entire class rose and greeted her with "Good Afternoon, Sr. Mary Noel. Please be seated." They then pointed to an empty chair. Sister said she never forgot such courtesy.

One photo in the Centennial book shows seven BVM Sisters standing behind two 7th grade boys in the "Going to the Mission Pageant". The boys are dressed in cassock and biretta[14] with a large cross hanging from their belt.

Lay People

If the vast majority of the 2,500 HOC families attended Sunday Mass in the 1950's, we should not assume that people lived on a higher moral level.

---

[14] The Biretta is a hard, square, ceremonial hat with three or four vertical projections and sometimes with a pompom or tassel at the top, worn by Roman Catholic clergy. It was originally a sign of office for Imperial Roman officials. Source: Webster's New World College dictionary, 4th Edition. © Macmillan, NY, NY

Attendance was demanded at risk of mortal sin; however, if you picked the right Mass, you could be there and back home in 45 minutes.

Traditional parish organizations thrived while Kathy and her sisters were growing up. Older women had the Altar & Rosary Society and the Mother's Club was a force for school volunteers and fund-raising. But make no mistake, the BVM Sisters ran the school with the motto: "If we want parental advice, we'll ask for it." And that was fine with most parents.

The Holy Name Society gathered monthly for Mass, followed by breakfast, and often a speaker. The Holy Name men also raised money and drove disabled adults to monthly services.

The 1940's and 1950's also saw the Our Sorrowful Mother novena movement in full swing. Novenas were said at different hours on first Friday afternoons and evenings for many years. Lines formed outside waiting to get in, especially during WW II.

Kathy's sister Patricia remembers that all the 6th, 7th, and 8th graders left HOC school at 3PM on to attend the novena for one hour as a group. Pat would then go to the local fish market to purchase the main course for Friday's dinner. She also remembers that some of the ladies who just left the novena would often push the kids aside to get to their fish order in first.

However, while the Lanes had a fish-dinner every Friday, someone often made a midnight run for B-B-Q Beef sandwiches from Russell's on North Avenue.

Christian Family Movement

In the 1960's, the Christian Family Movement (CFM) arrived at HOC. Teams of five to seven married couples would meet in each other's home every two weeks. Each group followed a common program of discussion. The first year's program covered scripture topics and the second covered current events. From discussion flowed actions like visiting a neighbor or writing a senator.

The Second Vatican Council

The Second Vatican Council (1962-1965) took place during the entire four years that Kathy and I were in high school. The Council and its aftermath had a far-reaching impact on the entire Catholic Church; but the highlights for laypeople sitting in the pew included[15]:

- Mass and other liturgies in English rather than Latin. Movement of the altar to allow the Eucharist celebrant to face the congregation. Women could attend church without covering their head.
- New open attitudes to other religions. Catholics permitted for the first time to attend weddings and funerals at other faiths.

---

[15] Source: Catholicism, New Edition; Richard P. McBrien, © 1994 Harper Collins, NY.

- Formally recognition of salvation outside the Church and the beginning Catholic involvement in the ecumenical movement.
- Active encouragement for laypeople to study the bible.
- Restoration of the Permanent Deaconate (after 1,400 years).
- Creation of two lay ministries, Lector and Eucharist Minister.
- Removal of serious penalties for Catholics who married "outside the Church" and before Protestant ministers.

While many felt Vatican II as a breath of 'fresh air' and while some of the changes were implemented quickly, many took 10-15 years to become a comfortable part of parish life.

Many clergy and laypeople felt uncomfortable or even threatened by the changes coming from Vatican II, not least of which were pastors trained in the 1930's or 1940's and who were often very comfortable with a 'top-down' authority model.

Chapter 6:

Young Kathy Lane

When Kathy was five her two sisters were attending Trinity High School in River Forest. Trinity was a girl's college preparatory school run by the Sinsinawa Dominican Sisters. Upwardly mobile Catholic families in Oak Park, River Forest and the Austin area of Chicago sent their daughters to Trinity. The sons went to Fenwick HS.

Being 10 and 12 years younger than her sisters, she still got a lot of attention from both. Patricia was more responsible and often looked after Kathy and helped her with her homework. Judy would later teach Kathy how to dance and smoke cigarettes.

Kathy also spent a great deal of time with her cousin Jack Hays. Jack was three years her senior and lived in the next parish, Our Lady of Angels.

Being basically an only child to middle age parents gave Kathy a different relationship with her parents. Beginning at age three Kathy began to join her parents for their annual Miami Beach vacation. We have several photos of young Kathy in Miami. We also have Christmas photos of Kathy in her cowgirl outfit surrounded by many toys and showing Uncle Tom Fitzmaurice holding her stuffed animals.

Kathy and her sisters didn't lack for much.

Harry's Illness

When Kathy was 10 her father had his first heart attack at age fifty. He would have several more before dying during her junior year of high school. Harry received great medical treatment from Frank Murphy

M.D. but there was really very little they could do to fight his type of heart disease.

Student Athlete

Like her father, Kathy became an avid reader. Harry had to borrow books from the Chicago Public Library because Kathy's age restricted her to the "children's room."

She was a bright student and received an excellent grammar school education, even with sixty kids per classroom and 1,600 students in the school. Kathy won the American Legion award for being the top girl student in her 8th grade class of 120 students.

POLIO

When Judy Lane entered high school in 1951, Poliomyelitis was a major fear among American parents. This infectious virus disease of the central nervous system struck approximately 60,000 children each year, resulting in serious paralysis conditions for about 1,000 children.

In 1955 Kathy Lane and Gene Flynn were among the first wave of children getting mass inoculations of the vaccine developed by Jonas Salk. By the time Kathy entered high school in 1961, outbreaks of this dreaded disease were falling to only a few cases a year.

Chicago 16-Inch Baseball

Kathy was very active in sports like swimming and baseball. Despite her slight size, she was quite good at baseball and very disappointed when her cousin Jack told her: "Baseball was really for boys." The fact that Kathy was often a better hitter might have had something to do with his statement and his frustration.

Despite any hard feelings she felt toward Jack that day, Kathy remained close to Jack the rest of her life.

Kathy and Jack played in 16-inch softball games; hardball and gloves were reserved for playing catch.

Sixteen-inch baseball was and is a native-Chicago specialty. All you needed was a moderate size lot (a basketball court plot of land would do), one 16-inch ball[16], two or three bats, and a bunch of kids. Gloves, protective gear, umpires, and parents were not required. A hit ball could even strike a parked or moving car without damage. When pressed, four kids could even play a version of 16-inch baseball in an alley,[17] with a pitcher and fielder on each team.

---

[16] One 16-inch ball could easily last five or more kids games. I recently saw a SportsMart advertisement for the ball in the Chicago Tribune. The $9.99 16-inch 'Clincher' softball was on sale for $7.99. A small note next to the price stated "Not available in Indiana".

[17] For the benefit of suburban readers, a Chicago alley was a narrow roadway that ran behind two rows of houses. The city lots were long and narrow, allowing for home or apartment near the front of the lot, a yard in the middle and a garage in the rear. The only way a car could reach the garage was via the alley. In winter snowstorms, alleys were seldom plowed, and one stuck auto could block all movement.

I played the same game in my Chicago neighborhood and at the Wisconsin lake community taken over by vacationing Chicagoans. Kids with very different ages and skills would choose up sides, and take the field. A team could even do without a catcher if short on players.

Pitching was underhand and balls and strikes were not called. If someone took too long to swing at a ball, the field would start shouting. The base path was short and runners could not leave the base until the ball was hit.

Usually it was pretty clear if a runner was safe or out. However, because the foul line was usually not clearly marked, calling a ball fair or foul became the biggest area of dispute. If a common agreement could not be reached the teams might decide to "play it over." Depending on the outcome of the replay, one team or the other might yell: "liars luck" or "cheaters proof."

Even in 2002 the Chicago Park District has a large program of <u>adult</u> 16-inch baseball leagues, but I am not sure how many kids still play the game unsupervised. As a society we don't have much trust in our kids doing group things without parents, rulebooks, and a formal appeals process.

Chicago's Finest

Richard J. Daley became Mayor of Chicago in 1956 and worked to improve services and consolidate his political base.

However, in January 1960 a major Police corruption scandal unfolded when a 23-year-old burglar in police custody confessed to burglarizing scores of homes with the help of twelve Summerdale District policemen. The officers even drove the loot away in police-cars. A search of the officer's homes confirmed the burglar's story.

Before his opponents could capitalize on the scandal, Mayor Daley appointed a "Blue-Ribbon" committee, lead by O.W. Wilson, to find a new police chief. The committee interviewed candidates for 28-days and then selected committee chairman Wilson for the job. Wilson was then Dean of the UCLA School of Criminology and the author of *Police Administration*, a leading police textbook.

Mayor Daley went along with the recommendation and Wilson became Police Commissioner. One of his first acts was to "clean house" and remove former Commissioner Tim O'Connor's inner team, including John Lane.

Mayor Daley asked John Lane to move to a position at O'Hare Airport. For some reason, John didn't want anything to do with O'Hare. Instead he spent a year at Chicago Department of Urban Renewal and then moved to the Chicago Board of Health as Chief Director of Finance.

O.W. Wilson went on to make many changes in the CPD, but none was more hated by the officers than switching from 2-man police cars to 1-man cars. This also affected my father, then a Traffic Accident Officer in the Lawndale district.

Party of the People

Harry Lane was a solid Democrat who believed that FDR and the New Deal saved the country. While he

44

worked for a conservative Chicago Tribune, he would often say: "Don't believe all you read on the editorial page, read columnists like Mike Royko first." In today's Tribune, Harry would probably recommend columnists like Bob Green and John Kass.

The Lane family followed with great interest John F. Kennedy's campaign for the presidency. Through his police friends, John Lane arranged for Kathy and her sisters to be standing in the back access hallway when JFK entered the Chicago Stadium for a rally two days before the November election. Kathy took a picture of the candidate, but it has faded with age.

On election night 13-year old Kathy and her dad stayed up all night to watch the returns come in. Richard Nixon would later claim that the Daley machine stole the election by withholding the Chicago count until they determined how many "ghost voters" were needed to win Illinois for Kennedy.

Harry always said Nixon got what he deserved.

Friendships

Kathy saw the great loyalty that her parents had to their friends and family. Harry took special care to include John's two daughters in fun activities.

Harry and Catherine would entertain Harry's priest classmates. The Lane apartment was a place where the classmates could come to for a good time among friends.

Kathy also saw her mother stay close to her sisters and friends despite occasional hard feelings and harsh words. Some of these women had a sharp tongue and sometimes were jealous of what they considered Catherine's easy life or the way the Lane girls were raised.

Sister Margaret in particular lived frugally despite her wealth from Sears Roebuck employment. One of her sayings was: "Never visit a doctor in a new dress, he might charge you more." Margurite thought that Harry and Catherine spent money far too freely. Ironical, by being childless, much of her money was later left to Catherine and further supported the spending habits she questioned.

Kathy's Friends

Kathy had many friends in grammar school. Judy Scornavacco and Martha Fowler were friends from Kindergarten to the end of her life.

Martha tells the story of eleven-year-old Kathy falling from a tree in the Fowler yard. Martha's mother saw the mishap and always claimed that Kathy's many illnesses began with the fall. Kathy, on the other hand, always thought that her bad back originated from a belly flop off the high-dive at a Miami Beach hotel. The swimming manager saw her land and insisted that this dangerous nine-year-old be given free diving lessons.

Kathy and her friends did not need organized sports. They had local lots for baseball and Lafollette Park for swimming in the summer and ice-skating in the winter.

Kathy and her Dad

Between the ten-year gap with her sisters and Harry's failing health, Kathy had a somewhat different father/daughter experience than Pat and Judy.

Kathy already shared a lot of Harry's values, including: love of knowledge, Chicago White Sox baseball, and friendship.

Harry's long illness also gave father and daughter time to talk. His illness also caused lot of frustrations for Kathy. It was very hard for her to understand Harry's mood swings. Fortunately, she and her friends could escape to her married sister Pat's near-by home.

Kathy learned much from her father, including fighting the good fight in the face of illness.

John Lane

In the late 1950's Harry Lane's heart condition was getting steadily worse. At the same time, a more outgoing John Lane seemed to be emerging even as Harry withdrew to a slower place.

John became the president of the Siena Father's Club, the high school his daughters Jacqueline and Barbara were attending. Jacqueline tells the story of the principal, Sr. Mary Inviolata, calling John to ask if he could find a Jukebox for the school cafeteria. A week later a jukebox was delivered to the school; it was probably confiscated by the Chicago Police during a vice raid. The sisters were delighted.

Sr. Mary Inviolata called to thank John, but also pointed out that the jukebox contained a number of records that were "totally inappropriate" for a Catholic high school. John was said to reply: "Sister, I got the jukebox, I think you should take care of the appropriate music."

John was never one for long discussions or chitchat.

Chapter 7:

Gene Flynn's Story

Like Kathy Lane, I was also part of a west side Irish Catholic family; fourth child of Frank and Mary Flynn.

My father was born in 1910. His father was a Chicago Police Captain (acting). When I was growing up, my paternal grandparents were already dead and we had relatively little contact with the Flynn relatives. Our family life focused much more on my mother's family of origin.

The Sullivan / Lyons Clan

My grandfather Roger Lyons was born in Chicago in 1894 to parents recently arrived from County Kerry in Ireland.

My grandmother Mary Sullivan was born in Reem, County Kerry in 1894 and left Ireland at age 16 to work as a live-in maid for a family in New York City. The mother of the house gave too many orders so Mary quit. She petitioned her priest Uncle Eugene Sullivan[18] to find her a job in Chicago. He did so, and she enjoyed working for the Strauss family until she and Roger Lyons married in 1914.

---

[18] Rev. Eugene Sullivan eventually became pastor of Resurrection Parish on Jackson Blvd. He was of the era when pastors were building larger and larger schools and churches to house the many families moving from the inner city to edges of the city. A story is told of a foreman coming to Msgr. Sullivan one morning to complain that vandals had knocked down a newly bricked wall for the 900-seat Resurrection Auditorium. Msgr. Sullivan was said to reply: "I did that myself, I expect your bricklayers to do a better job."

Roger became a Master plumber and helped build the Great Lakes Training Center near Waukegan. There was also plenty of construction work in the 1920's.

Roger and Mary had five children. Mary was the oldest, followed by Alice, Eugene (named in honor of Mary's uncle), Margaret, and Roger (named in honor of his father).

Sr. Margaret Lyons, RSM, recalls the family story that Roger and Mary loved Riverview Amusement Park on Western Avenue. As young parents, Roger and Mary would sneak out of the house whenever relatives came to visit. The relatives were stuck baby-sitting while Roger and Mary had fun at Riverview.

Like many other families, the Lyons family had a tough time in the 1930's. Roger had no work for several years and was happy to accept a low paying janitorial position at Resurrection parish. My mother, as the oldest child, put aside her dream of becoming a teacher[19] and went to work at the Montgomery Wards accounting department.

She and Police Officer Frank Flynn married in 1939. Mary was 23 and Frank 29.

Flynn Values

Mary was a very strong believer in security for her kids. She planned her daughters to become teachers and sons to become priests. When a high school teacher suggested that daughter Loretta was not

---

[19] Mary Flynn would later receive a BA degree from Roosevelt University, Chicago. While she never achieved her dream of becoming a teacher, she did become a Sr. Clerk in the Admissions Office of Chicago Loop College.

college material, Mary attacked with great vengeance. When my uncle Roger suggested to me that there were careers other than priesthood, Mary told him bluntly to mind his own business.

Mary made essentially all the key decisions for the Flynn family, while Frank provided the emotional support for the kids. He loved being our dad and told us so all the time.

In hindsight, Mary showed her love by getting us ready for college and saving the money that allowed us to go. In my memory, kind words and warm hugs were not a big part of her style.

Schooling

The Flynn children attended Resurrection School on Jackson Blvd. My older brother Jim excelled at sports and academics while I struggled with many subjects, especially spelling. I remember Mary spending countless hours drilling me in that subject. In fourth grade I came home with the proud announcement that my teacher told me that I was the "smartest one in the dumb row!"

In what we now call Junior high, my life finally moved beyond the tragedy of spelling deficiency. Sister Mary Catherine Daly (Sr. Devota) RSM saw that I was good at math and moved me into the math "high track."

Summers and Scouting

I also joined the Boy Scouts for winter activities and began to spend the entire summer at the summer home my parents owned with uncle Rev. Eugene Lyons. My grandmother was there all summer and my parents would come up on weekends.

When I first joined the Scouts I picked up my uniform and my 12-inch forest knife. My father was concerned with my carrying such a dangerous looking weapon. Mary however, would allow no discussion saying: "of course Gene needs the knife, its part of the Boy Scout kit."

The Value of the Dollar

Mary wanted her sons to know how to manage money. When I was in 5th grade I took over my bother's *Austin News* paper-route. For the next four years I delivered the paper each Wednesday afternoon after school. My friend Ray Williams delivered the *Austin Night* with essentially the same news to the same group of customers. We both collected the money as well. And with a monthly subscription of $.15, most people gave us $.25 and told us to keep the change. At Christmas time, a tip of $.50 or $1.00 was common.

Our Lady of Angels Fire

I was making my *Austin News* collection rounds on December 1st, 1958 and told a number of customers of the fire that afternoon at Our Lady of Angels School. Three BVM sisters and 97 students lost their lives.

Many of the injured children were taken to Saint Ann's hospital. My policeman father was on duty directing traffic around the hospital that night. He saw hundreds of parents looking for their children, unsure if they were alive or dead.

OLA was the parish next to HOC. After the fire, Kathy Lane and all the HOC students ended classes each day at noon to allow OLA kids to use the same classrooms. Kathy got to know some of the OLA survivors at Siena and Mundelein College.

On to the High School Seminary

I entered high school at Quigley South and like my brother, I moved in with my grandparents on Jackson Blvd, across from Resurrection Church. Living there gave easy access to the 6:30 AM Mass and the Congress rapid-transit line.

I finally took charge of my own study assignments and to actually begin to read books. After Sunday dinner, my uncle Fr. Gene Lyons would help me with my Latin studies. While I would never excel at Latin, Fr. Gene made me feel good about working on it.

As in Harry Lane's day, Quigley had a great faculty of priests and now laypeople. My own growing maturity, and faculty encouragements, helped me gain much more confidence in myself. By third year I was in the advanced group for several subjects. Making new friends and taking ski trips actually brought some fun to my life.

Like Kathy Lane, my father died during my junior year of high school. To this day I am thankful that he often told us all of his love for us. I also appreciate that he worked as a policeman in tough areas without becoming bitter or hateful toward minorities.

College

By the time I finished Quigley, seminary students no longer went directly to the major seminary at Mundelein, Illinois. Instead, we spent two years at Niles College, where my uncle Eugene Lyons, was President and Rector.

Gene Lyons showed me the same style and grace here as he had tutoring me in high school Latin. In later years I was honored to serve with my brother as Trustee for Gene's trust during the last ten years of his life.

My two years at Niles College and the two years at the major seminary were a great experience. I made great friendships; had a lot of fun; and, except for Latin and Greek, had very good success in my course work. I also began to take some risks like joining a Fair-Housing march with Dr. Martin Luther King.

I left the major seminary after I got my BA degree. By that point I knew that the priesthood was not the right choice for me. I spent that summer working as a community organizer on the southwest side of Chicago. Without well-defined career goals I went off to graduate school at Northern Illinois University in August 1969.

I would meet Kathy Lane three months later. She found a young man that shared many of the same values she had gained from her father: concern for people, for social justice and for Chicago. Gene was even a White Sox fan.

Kathy often said that had Harry and Gene ever met, they would have liked each other.

Family of Origin

Kathy and I both came from west-side Irish Catholic families that valued education. However, our families had very different styles. In times of crisis, Harry Lane usually came up with a plan and got Catherine's "OK" before proceeding. In the Flynn home, Mary came up with the plan knowing that Frank would go along with it.

In times of crisis, married couples usually revert to the decision pattern of their childhood homes. In our case, I would wait for Kathy to take the lead and she would wait for me to come up with the plan. Needless to say, this was one of several issues that we had to work through early in our marriage.

Chapter 8:

Kathy's Story: High School & College

The Lane family belonged to Our Lady Help of Christians Parish, commonly called just HOC. The Church sat in the middle of a 1.5 square mile boundary. Most of the parishioners could walk three – five blocks to the Church.

Except for trips to department stores in Oak Park or the Chicago Loop, people shopped locally. Supermarkets were just starting to appear around Chicago, but the Lanes believed in shopping at small privately owned food stores and butcher shops.

After school, Kathy and Judy Scornavacco worked as a cashier at the Stella Brothers Food Store on Division Street. One of their duties was walking the store looking for people stealing cans of food; they didn't find a single thief.

High School

Kathy did not follow her sisters to Trinity HS in River Forest. Wanting to be different, she chose Siena High School run by the Religious Sisters of Mercy. Siena was a Catholic Girls High School that had both secretarial and college preparation programs. The school had some great teachers, but on average offered a weak preparation of college.

Attending Siena allowed Kathy to excel in studies and sports, but left her behind the academic curve when she got to College.

HOC Teens

However, much of Kathy's life revolved outside of Siena. She was very active in the Help of Christians (HOC) parish teen club that was under the direction of Father Tony Clare, a young and dynamic priest. Kathy, along with Judy Scornavacco, Martha Fowler, Patricia Mooney, Tom Gibbons, Jay Krakora, Delany and four or five others were a team unto themselves.

Kathy met Carole Gogin at Siena; Carole became an active member of the HOC team by reason of her staying at Kathy's home a lot of the time. Tom Gibbons was also a regular at the Lane house, even if Kathy was gone. Harry and Catherine welcomed all who came to their door.

One photo shows Kathy and Jay Krakora cooking dinner for the team on a Wisconsin camping trip. The Krakora station wagon and camper can be seen in the background. On this same trip, another teen got the station wagon stuck between two trees while Tom Gibbons was teaching her to drive.

Kathy gave a helping hand to many of her friends. They repaid it in kind during school years and for the rest of their lives. As Martha Campbell said recently, "We weren't into photos so much in high school." I am not sure if photos would tell the story, even if they did exist.

Teenage life:

In the 50's and 60's high school students could hangout together locally or hop on a CTA bus to attend an event in another part of Chicago. Until the late-60's, almost no one had a car of their own and most families had only one automobile.

During summer vacation, many HOC teens worked in downtown Chicago and rode the Lake Street El to get there. Patricia Lane worked downtown at the Fair Store one year and at the Sears store the next. Kathy Lane spent one Christmas season working after school at Marshall Fields. She recalled selling a mink jacket to the wife of a Chicago TV personality. The jacket was a gift for the family's small dog.

High School boys could often summer work in one of the many local factories, filling in for workers on vacation. I worked at a paper-converting factory one summer and at the Brach Candy factory another. It was an eye-opening experience.

Harry's Health Declines

Harry's health continued to decline while Kathy started high school. Uncle John Lane taught her to drive as he did for Pat and Judy Lane. While Harry still kept his advertising business going he would tire very easily.

Once a year he had to go to Detroit for advertising events at the Detroit Auto Show. On several of these trips, his nephew Jack Hays drove. I am sure that Harry used these trips to share ideas on many topics, including the value of a Jesuit education.

Harry Lane died, at age 58, during Kathy's junior year of High School. Twenty-five priests were at the altar; many of them were Harry's Seminary classmates.

Pat and Judy were already married by that time. Kathy's aunt Marie Fitzmaurice had also died several years earlier. By now, Aunt Vic, her husband John, and son Jack lived in Marie's old apartment, one floor above Kathy's and her mom's apartment.

Proms

Kathy lead a very active social live. In senior year she attended three Proms in addition to the Siena Prom. The Siena Prom concluded with breakfast for eight couples back at the Lane apartment. Everyone came except Kathy and her date; they lingered at the shores of Lake Michigan to watch sunrise.

Kathy's mom, now a widow, took all this in stride. Catherine had a good sense of fun and trust in her daughter.

To the BVM Novitiate and Back

In senior year of high school, Kathy decided she wanted to join the BVM sisters. This came as a surprise to BVM Sister Ruth Schiffler. Sr. Ruth had taught Kathy at HOC and had stayed close to the Lane family while Kathy was in high school. Sr. Ruth remembers Kathy as having an unusually strong character under a quiet, unassuming personality.

After graduating from Siena, Kathy enjoyed her summer and prepared to enter the BVM order. She was to spend her Novitiate year at the BVM Motherhouse in Dubuque, Iowa.

I always thought that joining the convent was a deathbed request by Harry Lane. Kathy's aunt Vic thought that one of the BVM sisters was the main proponent. However, Martha Fowler and Sister Ruth thought Kathy had made her own decision to join the BVMs.

Martha was saddened at Kathy's pending departure, but her mother told her: "Don't be sad, a home-sick Kathy will be back in no time."

In any case, Kathy and her mom packed a huge ocean-liner trunk with everything she would need for the next year. On a sunny August Saturday, Kathy's mom and friends saw her off from a downtown Chicago train station. Everyone was upset with Kathy's departure.

As it happens, Sr. Ruth also went to Dubuque the next day and was there the following Wednesday when the postulant mistress called to say that Kathy wanted to talk to her. In a tearful voice, Kathy said: "I don't think I can live this life. But I don't want to disappoint you or my mother." Sr. Ruth replied: "That's what you came to find out and it would be an injustice to you and the Congregation to stay when it wasn't you vocation." Sr. Ruth told her to call her mother and ask her to come for her.

Kathy kept her pledge of trying the novitiate. However, Mrs. Fowler's comment proved true, a home-sick Kathy was back in Chicago a week after she left.

There are, however, two lasting results of her trip to Iowa:

- It changed Kathy's relationship with aunt Vic.

Kathy came back with <u>many</u> complaints about life at the BVM novitiate. When her mother would listen no more, Kathy went upstairs to aunt Vic's apartment. Vic listened and listened, which helped Kathy get it out of her system. Vic would later say that her very close relationship with Kathy began that August. And that relationship extended to David when Vic and John became his active grandparents.

- The ocean-liner trunk still resides in the basement of our Kildeer home.

College Days

Kathy was back from the novitiate in time to enter Mundelein College in September 1965, the same year I started at Niles College of Saint Mary of the Lake Seminary. Mundelein College was a well-respected liberal arts college for women run by the BVM order. The focal point of the college was an imposing 19-story Skyscraper building next to Loyola University of Chicago's Lakeshore campus. A new library overlooking Lake Michigan had just opened before Kathy got there.

Kathy drove her Chevy Monza (the car Ralph Nader tagged "Unsafe at any speed") to Mundelein College each day. Kathy got a great education there and did very well in any class that called for creative thinking and writing skills. Don't ask about science and math.

Kathy and her friends were also regulars at Hamilton's Bar on Sheridan Road.

Collection of Thoughts

Kathy contracted Tuberculosis (TB)[20] during the second half of her freshman year (1966) and spent three months in home confinement. My father had also contracted TB and spent four months in a Chicago TB Sanitarium in late 1961.

Kathy's confinement gave her a chance to read many books; some became life-long favorites.

Kathy also started a journal she called a "collection of thoughts of other people's and my own." The words of poets, songwriters, civil-rights leaders, friends and even her father are found there. Her friend Patricia Moody and songwriter Rod McKune were frequent contributors. Some entries include:

Recorded September 6, 1965: "If one is out of touch with oneself; then one cannot touch others." (Ann-Marie Lindbergh's *Gift from the Sea*)

"Never lower yourself to any man by raising yourself up. But don't hesitate to put a hand down and pull someone up." (dad)

April 29, 1968: "Public service is exciting because you're involved in things other than

---

[20] Like Polio, Tuberculosis is an infectious disease and was a major health problem until antibiotics were discovered in the early 1940's. Deaths from TB in the United States dropped from 188 per 100,000 deaths in 1904 to about 1 per 100,000 in 1980. Source: Microsoft Encarta Encyclopedia 1998

yourself. If you just sit and worry about your own problems, you can get very sick." (Robert Kennedy)

May 27, 1968: "Life is perhaps the effort given to making memories. We all want to be remembered and we all want to have moments which we can remember!" (KL)

June 6, 1968: "the day Bobby Kennedy went home."

The Times they are a changing

The second half of the 1960's brought major changes to college campuses across America, including:

- Campus participation in the Civil Rights movement was winding down and anti-war activities were on the upswing. In 1964 Mundelein sent a bus of students and faculty to join the Selma Alabama freedom march; by 1967, anti-war protests with Loyola students were the rage.

- Many students were angry that college administrations were slow to embrace the anti-Vietnam war movement. At Mundelein College, someone showered buckets of red paint on the two 25-foot tall stone angels that stood at the entrance to the main building. What a powerful message: "…let the blood be on your wings."

- In 1967, the San Francisco "summer of love" was flourishing at Haight-Asbury and became a cultural phenomenon at many campuses.

Kathy did not play an active role in the civil-rights struggle or the emerging anti-Vietnam protests. She did, however, get involved in the political campaign of Robert Kennedy in the spring of 1968. She spent at least one weekend working in Hammond, Indiana for the Kennedy campaign. I was there too, but we didn't meet.

Other Changes and End of an Era

While the civil rights and antiwar movements were very visible and dramatic, other significant changes were taking place in Chicago and most large American cities:

- The residents of "urban villages" like HOC were rapidly moving to the suburbs. Chicago reached its population peak of 3.6 million in 1950.[21] By 1990, the city population had fallen to 2.8 million. During the same 40-year span, the suburban population grew from 2.8 million to 4.6 million.

- Beginning in the early 1970s, the Catholic Church in American began to see both a dramatic drop in the number of young men

---

[21] US Census: 1950 and 1990.

entering major seminaries, and a dramatic increase in men leaving the priesthood. For example, in 1967 Jim Flynn was ordained for the Archdiocese of Chicago in a near-record size class of 50. Not only did 30 of the 50 ordained leave the priesthood (15 alone in the 1970s); ordination classes after 1967 dropped steadily in size. By the late 1980's, the average ordination class for Chicago was twelve.

By the late 1970's it was clear to many that the era of large city parishes with overflowing schools and crowed convents and rectories was largely coming to an end.

Less clean was what its replacement would look like.

Ending Mundelein for Now

Kathy's class graduated from Mundelein in June 1969. She was not among the graduates due to the lost time with TB and the need to repeat several science classes. She left college anyway and went to work at the Chicago Board of Health.

Chicago Board of Health

Uncle John Lane got Kathy a job at the Chicago Board of Health, where he was the power behind the nominal head. The Board of Health had their own rules, and Kathy qualified for one of the many categories of Social Worker.

She worked with a program that went to grammar schools to test children for heart murmurs. Children with serious conditions were offered free surgery by great surgeons. Kathy's job was to work with the parents to ensure they understood and supported the surgery. Kathy had a great knack for making parents comfortable with the program even if they didn't trust city government or Cook County Hospital.

Kathy worked with a group as diverse as Chicago itself. Kathy reported to Raphie, a Berlin-trained social worker and Nazi concentration camp survivor. Angie, Willie, and Wauneta were Nurses, and Ruth Rosenthal became Kathy's on-the-job friend.

When work for the school-screening program was light, Kathy and Ruth assisted Dr. Jeremiah Stamler, M.D. in his research of the relationship between blood cholesterol and heart disease. Dr. Stamler was on the faculty of Northwestern University Medical School and a leading researcher on the effects of cholesterol.

Dr. Stamler was also noted for his stand at refusing to testify before the US House Committee for Un-American Activities[22] (HUAC). Many people, including Kathy, saw this committee as follow-on to the McCarthy committee Communist witch hunts of early 1950's.

Kathy had great respect for Dr. Stamler as a doctor, a researcher, and as a man who stood by his principles.

---

[22] Movie fans can see a very realistic portrayal of HUAC in the 2001 Warner Brothers movie *The Majestic* staring Jim Carrey.

Full Circle for the Lane Brothers

Everyone knew that Kathy was niece to John Lane, but once they got to know her, they didn't hold it against her.

John told Kathy to work hard and stay out of trouble. He also helped her purchase a new car from a dealer that did business with the city. Kathy wanted a convertible, but John would not hear of it. She got a sporty but safer Malibu.

Kathy stayed close to John and would stop into his office from time to time. One morning she mentioned that her new car was at the dealers for two days of repairs. John picked up the phone and told the owner of the dealership: "If Kathy's car wasn't ready by 5:00 PM that evening, a brick would be thrown through his window that night."

John had a temper and wanted to remind the owner, in his own way, that he expected a high level of service for Kathy. He also knew that the car would be ready at 5:00 PM, and it was.

Life for the Lane brothers had come full circle. Where Harry Lane tried to look after John's two daughters in the past; John was now looking after Harry's youngest daughter.

Kathy would later joke that John probably ran a background check on Gene Flynn. I am sure it wasn't a joke to John and I bet he was pleased to see I had a Chicago Policeman father.

Chapter 9:

Gene and Kathy – The Early Years

The Wedding

We married on October 16, 1971 at Saint Vincent Ferrer Church in River Forest. Kathy walked down the long isle with uncle John Lane.

Rev. Tom Murphy, later Bishop of Seattle, helped us plan the wedding but stayed in the background during the ceremony. Rev. Charlie Osweiler concelebrated the Mass with my brother Jim and uncle Msgr. Gene Lyons.

Gene Lyons gave the homily. And while Gene was usually listed as one of the best speakers among Chicago priests, he was off that day. His homily included a discussion of the current Chicago City Hall racetrack scandal.

John Peterson, a friend from my seminary days, played the guitar and sang some of our 1960's favorites like *Kumbya*. John also sang the recently released *Wedding Song* by Paul Stookey[23]. It's a great song with the 2nd stanza speaking to the joint journey of life.

We had a great wedding reception at the Marriott O'Hare hotel. Mike Curtin later drove Kathy and me back to her mom's apartment to change for our honeymoon trip. We spent the night back at the Marriott hotel before flying off to Jamaica.

The Marriott hotel was also hosting to a VFW convention that weekend; the ex-soldiers wished us well as we took a cab to the airport.

---

[23] Paul wrote the song for Peter Yarrow's 1971marriage ceremony. Peter and Paul made up 2/3 of the Peter, Paul and Mary folk singing group. For lyrics for this and other PP&M songs, see www.peterpaulandmary.com

Ringing in 1972

At least two of Kathy's HOC friends had also married in 1971. Judy Scornavacco married Jim Hoffman and Martha Fowler married Lt. David Campbell, recently returned from Vietnam. Tom and Nancy Gibbons as well as Jay and Mary Sue Krakora also lived nearby. Each wedding shows a group photo of HOC teens and spouses. Only Martha and Dave lived away from Chicago, moving from one US Army base to another every two years.

Kathy and I rented a two-bedroom apartment on Madison Street in River Forest. The 2nd bedroom became an office with a pullout couch for nieces and nephews that came to visit.

We hosted a large New Years-Eve party. All our friends came and celebrated into the early hours of the New Year.

Fifteen-minutes after the last of the guests had left, we got a panic phone call from Nancy Gibbons. She told us they had lost her husband on the drive home with Judy and Jim Hoffman. Tom had stepped out of the car on Chicago Avenue because he was feeling ill and was nowhere to be found.

Kathy and I drove over to join the search. We pictured Tom asleep under some bush. The Oak Park police suggested that it would be better if we found him before they did.

As it turns out, Tom had walked four blocks east and was having breakfast at the Rex, a restaurant open 24-hours a day.

Through this adventure and several joint vacation trips I was becoming a full member of Kathy's HOC team. As an adult, I picked up much of what I missed in High School.

Youth Baseball

Kathy volunteered to teach CCD at Help of Christians Parish and I managed the T-Ball team of our nephew Mike Janowiak.

Every team has at least one kid that can't play baseball well. The one on our team would always strike out, which is hard to do in T-Ball. In game ten, our weak hitter finally got a hit and stood proudly on 1st base. His M.D. father ran from the sidelines and instead of hugging his child, he shouted: "Finally, you didn't let your team down!"

I also had two assistant coaches, Bill and Tom, working with the team. Bill wanted his son to be the "superstar of T-Ball" by keeping him in T-Ball a second year. Tom also took T-Ball baseball very seriously; we nearly had to call the paramedics twice because he started to hyperventilate.

If the kids stopped to think about it, they would probably conclude that their role was to prevent embarrassment and promote the glory of their parents.

Eighteen years into the future our son David would play in the Lake Zurich Youth Baseball program. He was very fortunate to have coaches like Jerry Micrut and Terry Nutter, coaches who believed that the kids were there to have fun and learn about teamwork. Parental glory was not part of the program.

Work & Study

I worked downtown at the Illinois Department of Labor and taught Sociology one night a week at Loyola University. Kathy continued to work for the Chicago Board of Health during our first years of marriage.

In late1973 I changed jobs and began to work at Rockwell International MGD Graphics division, where Bob Janowiak (husband to Kathy's sister Pat) was VP. I also began work on an MBA at the University of Chicago. I drove from work in Downers Grove to the John Hancock area for classes one or two nights a week.

Kathy and I spent lots of good times with friends and played a lot of tennis. We went to visit the Curtin home almost weekly. We did our laundry there and Judy made delicious barbequed ribs on many occasions. In 1976 Judy and Mike lent us their new Chevy station wagon for a Flynn/Hoffman/Gogin trip to Cape Code.

Frustrations

Our first years of marriage had many blessings and some real frustrations. I loved Kathy, but often put up an emotional wall between us. It took me a couple years of counseling with Dr. Rigoberto Rodriguez to uncover and resolve my angers toward my mother. Rather than express my anger to Mary, I was punishing Kathy via the emotional wall.

In hindsight, I think Kathy knew before we got married that it would take me a while to get up to speed on this adult man/woman thing. She knew that I had only three months of dating experience when we first met. I am very thankful that Dr. Rodriguez was there to help me and that he was able to talk to Kathy along the way.

Waiting for Baby

In early 1975 we were still not pregnant and began working with a leading fertility specialist recommended by Dr. Murphy. This was before many of the new options were available. The medical treatment consisted of different medicines that usually made Kathy very tearful.

I found the following note in Kathy's "Words of Wisdom" journal. While I don't recall us going to church much those years, Kathy's faith and thoughtfulness are very evident:

March 25, 1975

It's one of those nights where sleep will not come. Gene is in Canada (lucky Canada) and not even the rosary beads have been soothing enough to get me through the night. Perhaps putting thoughts to words will help.

I think I'm beginning to understand the word 'lonely' a little better now that Gene is traveling. At least that's the closest feeling I can think of to describe the little surge of emptiness I feel when he's gone.

I tried to explain to someone today a part of what my feeling for our marriage is – belief in one another. That person thought I was intellectualizing, and maybe that's right. But it was a nice feeling that I got while doing it.

Sometimes it still amazes me when I realize how much I've come to love Gene. It wasn't so much that our love has grown as it's expanded. There are times when I fear feeling so sure of something! (A throw back to the Puritan ethic?)

Tomorrow is another trip to the fertility doctor. So much depends on what he can do for us! Gene will make such a wonderful father. I feel like the inventor who has everything but his tools. Not that we will be perfect parents, but certainly we will try hard enough.

Sometimes lately I'm beginning to feel a pang of envy every time I see a child – must see the feeling for what it is and keep it to a minimum. Envy conceives nothing but more envy and bitterness.

I thank God that all levels of communication in our marriage have been open as regards this subject – one of our greatest blessings.

Communication is certainly lacking in many today. Just the ability to express ourselves in words has begun to suffer in today's society. Those who deal with the public should always speak plainly. Lincoln was a master of simple words.

Looking forward to Easter! Family gatherings have really become a joy (perhaps a sign of growing older) lately, and having everyone here together will I hope, be another successful first in our marriage. The nieces and nephews are growing so fast – and each in a unique way. Another grand feeling just talking to Cathy Curtin the other day. I mean really talking. She has a inquisitive mind and a real instinct for topics which are philosophically deep. I think she is learning the principal of one question more than likely leads to another rather than to a nice 'pat answer'.

I hope Gene is able to get home tomorrow. I know he'll try. I am anxious for us to start planning our Easter trip. - KLF

After 18 months of working with the fertility specialist, we decided to end the effort. We looked into adoption with Catholic Charities, but feared that Kathy's medical conditions would stand in the way of success.

On the Road to Mayo Clinic

By 1977 I was doing well in sales at Data General, a mini-computer company that competed with Digital Equipment. Kathy was working on finishing her BA degree at Mundelein College. She was also suffering from Inflammatory Bowel Disease (IBD).

The IBD condition was a growing problem. Kathy had Rheumatoid Arthritis since her late teens and IBD often occurs in patients with that type of arthritis. The local specialists tried a number of treatments, including a new one called "Hyperall."

The treatment involved giving the patient's bowel a total rest by feeding all needed nutrients via a tube that connected to a large artery. The process ran 12 hours a day under the management of a IVAC unit, the same unit that controls the medicines in those dripping bags within hospital rooms.

Kathy was one of the first patients in the Chicago area to have the whole setup outside a hospital setting. She was pretty good with the cumbersome process for the first few weeks, but by the third week, she felt like the IVAC unit was controlling her life. She tossed it against the wall a couple of times; it proved remarkably durable.

In April 1977 we left for the Mayo Clinic in Rochester, MN. There is a great photo of Kathy behind the wheel of our green MG-B. The Mayo doctors confirmed that Kathy had IBD and called it the Crohns version. Unfortunately, they didn't have much to offer that the Chicago doctors hadn't tried. The condition seemed to come and go on its own terms, with fall and spring being more severe.

Matters of Trust

Kathy and I were very fortunate in the level of trust we had for each other. This trust was often subject-specific. For example, when she said that our relationship was in trouble I took it very seriously. When I said that our finances were a mess, she trusted my judgment. After all, she knew much more about relationships and I knew much more about investing.

Kathy hated to fly and was always nervous when I was off flying for business. If we were flying together, she felt a little better, trusting my judgment and knowing that we were together. Only once did this take us close to harm's way.

In 1978 we were traveling to Grand Bahamas Island to attend a company award event. We had landed in West Palm Breach, Florida to connect with a Delta flight to our destination.

When Delta announced that the flight was canceled and passengers would be bussed to Miami for a later flight, I started to look for an alternate airline. I was fortunate to get the last two seats on All-Caribbean Airlines. When Kathy asked if the 4-propeller airplane was safe, a doctor from Canada assured us that the deHavilland Otter was a great plane and used all the time "up north."

A few minutes later the pilot came over to the nineteen waiting passengers and explained that two of four electric starters were not working. He told us that he was going to take-off without passengers using two engines, "jump-start" the remaining engines and land to pick up the passengers. The only dicey part was boarding while all the engines were running.

Off we flew into the darkening sky. The pilot later told us that he was looking forward to his first night landing. We think he was only kidding.

Cruising

Our life together was beginning to settle into a comfortable routine. After Kathy finished her BA degree, she worked on a novel about an Irish family living in Chicago. I got my MBA degree in 1977. That gave us more time to vacation. We took a 10-day trip to San Francisco in the summer of 1977.

Kathy also began working as a reporter for a local weekly newspaper. She covered events like the Sleepy Hollow School Board meetings. She would come home from the meetings about 11:00 PM and write her articles over the next three hours. We were surprised at how few changes the editors made (none).

We thought we were cruising along pretty nicely. Little did we know that big changes were around the bend.

Chapter 10:

After David

In the fall of 1980 Kathy's OB-GYN performed a D&C procedures to address some menstrual irregularities. To his surprise, he found an undetected cyst on her uterus. Within three months we were pregnant.

Pregnancy is often helpful for people that suffer from IBD. In Kathy's case, she got this benefit and the disease never seemed to come back with the same intensity.

One photo shows Kathy in a maternity outfit. We were waiting for the promised "Thanksgiving baby" that arrived on Christmas day, 1981.

It is very natural for us to look at our married life as Before David and After David. He was the joy of our life and the gathering point for cousins, aunts and uncles.

4th of July

During several years in the late 1970's John and Mildred Lane hosted a 4th of July party for Lane and Fitzmaurice families. We all had a great time.

Between John's aging and the arrival of David, Kathy and I started to host the annual event. As we prepared the Palatine home and later the Kildeer home for the event, I took extra care that the grass and bushes would achieve the 'John Lane' level of quality.

With the strong encouragement of Jacqueline Lane Niesen we took an annual group photograph. We have about fifteen of these photos; they show the growth of

David and his cousins, some now with spouses. They also show the arrival of grandchildren for Judy Curtin and Jacqueline. The aging of the senior family members is also quite clear.

The 4th of July event and a Christmas season event in honor of David's birthday brought the family together. It also helped forge a close friendship between Kathy and Jacqueline Lane Niesen.

In future years the two annual events at the Flynn's home gave family members a chance to spend quality time with other family members.

David's First Year

Kathy stayed home with David while I began a new job selling for a start-up company called Stratus Computer. Our beloved green MG-B convertible was traded in for VW-Rabbit that could hold Kathy, David and some groceries.

Florida Vacations

In January 1983, the three of us took our first family vacation to Jupiter, Florida, along the Atlantic coast. The photos show large waves, seagulls and sunburned son. One of the photos is on the cover of this book.

David cried whenever he was on the sand - until we learned that he loved to sit under a cabana. The cabana gave warmth and shelter from the wind. The Florida vacation became a Flynn annual event.

When Dave was eight we switched to the Gulf side of Florida. Friends told us of a quiet resort called "Palm Island" near Englewood, Florida. We would take the ferryboat from the mainland to a small island with one restaurant, no cars, no golf course, and housing units built on stilts near the water.

Palm Island became our spring break home-away-from-home. We were all altogether in a relaxing environment. It usually worked that my birthday and the Oscar awards took place during our Florida week; this only added to the fun.

Kathy did not get homesick during these trips; but she did miss our dogs.

Breast Cancer

We were just starting to talk about a second child when Kathy found a lump on her left breast. While the doctors assured us that it was most likely benign, a biopsy confirmed that the lump was cancerous. Kathy underwent a mastectomy in March 1983. Radiation or chemotherapy was not recommended.

New Job and New Home

In April I left Stratus Computer and returned to Digital Equipment. Working in a high-pressure start-up company with a young baby and cancer recovery was a bad combination.

Returning to Digital turned out extremely well. I held a new position as Sales Executive for the recently formed Ameritech. It was a great success almost from the start. Kathy and I went to Hawaii, San Diego and Europe on award trips. Even with the company travel, we took our annual winter trip to Florida.

In the 1970's and '80 many white-collar workers believed that if you worked hard, the company "would look after you." Kathy was very skeptical of this and other beliefs in "benevolent" corporate behavior. She supported my choice of working in technology sales because I loved to sell. At the same time she challenged me by saying: "Don't be naive, you are treated very well because you are a top producer."

We moved to Kildeer in 1985, after I overcame my hesitation of leaving our Palatine house with its low mortgage payment. Even though I was resentful of my mother's lack of emotional support, I shared some of her frugal habits. Kathy and I would joke that based on our childhoods, her ideal car was a Mercedes Benz and mine was a used Saturn. Somehow, we were always able to find some common ground.

Our Kildeer home had small forest of the backyard and ponds across the street. It had plenty of room for flowers and a wooden yard-gym for David. And while David complained that the area lacked sidewalks, it was our sanctuary even before the moving boxes were unpacked.

Kathy even loved to cut the grass on our lawn-tractor. The tractor also had a snow-thrower option that unfortunately required great patience to work properly. Once Kathy attacked a 3-inch snowfall while I was in Boston. She called to tell me "YOUR (blank) tractor has slid off the driveway into the rain gully". When I suggested she call AAA to get a free tow; she replied: "No way! You're going to pay through the nose for this."

A week later we signed up with a local snowplow service.

Cancer Reoccurrence

In November 1986, Kathy found a lump on her left chest wall. She had a second surgery and we began to work with Leon Dragon M.D., an Oncologist that had just moved from New York to St. Joseph Hospital in Chicago. Dr. Dragon recommended radiation therapy and gave us a letter for the Radiologist at the hospital close to our home.

We opened the letter and read with great shock that Kathy's type of Cancer Reoccurrence had a 90% chance of becoming systemic.

On our next visit to Dr. Dragon, we asked about the 90% risk factor. He said that the 90% risk occurs if no radiation therapy takes place and that the risk should be much lower in Kathy's case.

This was the beginning of a long relationship with Dr. Dragon. He proved to be a doctor of great skill, vigilance and care. He later treated Kathy's cousin Bunny and sister Judy.

Kathy did have the radiation therapy and Judy Curtin quit her job to allow her to watch David while Kathy received treatment four days a week for five weeks.

We have a picture from that time with Judy holding David and Cabbage Patch doll Wade Sidney.

Many people talk of love and charity; Judy lived it and was always there for her younger sister. I will always remember the rib-dinners when we were first married and Judy holding David and Wade Sidney.

Curtin Kids

Kathy and I stayed very close to Judy and her five children.

Ed lived with us after high school when he wasn't at college or in the army. While actually twenty years older than our son David, Ed could switch with remarkable ease between the role of caring uncle and fun loving brother. His moving to Colorado and marriage to Cheryl only strengthen the bonds to David and us.

Susan Curtin lived near us and talked to Kathy at least weekly; in many ways her relationship with Kathy came to parallel the close relationship Kathy had with aunt Vic. Susan also joined us on many of our Florida vacations.

We also watched with pride the way Nancy raised daughter Jamie as a single mom.

We saw less of Cathy and Tom because they lived out-of-state, but they did their best to attend the Flynn 4th of July event and were always at the Christmas get-together.

In the future, Cathy, Tom, Susan, Ed and Nancy would have to face their mom dying of leukemia and their dad dying to cancer within an 18-month period. It was not an easy time, but they stayed together.

Children the Challenge

Dave went to the Long Grove Montessori School (LGMS) near our new home. If he ever runs for president he can say he started his education in a one-room school just like Abe Lincoln. Margaret and Bob Riley owned the school and their love and commitment to the children came through in everything they did. They were in their mid-70s at the time and more active than most 40-year-olds I know.

Kathy and I became very involved with the school, especially when we signed on to help lead the effort to add a 1st thru 6th grade program. Kathy was the first president of the Parents Board. We were even thinking we should purchase the School if the Riley's ever decide to sell.

During this period we took a parenting course at LGMS called *Children the Challenge*[24]. The course was lead by local psychologist Kevin O'Connor, a friend and classmate from my seminary days. His sister was a BVM sister that taught Kathy at Mundelein.

The course covered many practical topics like " Don't turn your child's problem into your problem." But a core theme was the need to give our children "roots and wings." Roots to know who they are and wings to take off on their own.

Kathy gave this a lot of thought because, after the cancer reoccurrence, she felt that the odds of her seeing David graduate from High School or even grammar school were not great.

With the help of many people, Dave did develop a great sense of roots and wings. We were delighted to see our 5th grader fly to Washington, DC on his own to visit Martha and David Campbell. In 7th grade he began to make an annual trip to Colorado to visit cousin Ed Curtin and his wife Cheryl.

---

[24] Based on book *Children the Challenge,* Rudolf Dreikurs, © 1964, Plume Book, NY, NY

Tennis

Kathy loved to play tennis. It gave her a great workout and satisfied her competitive instincts. Kathy and I were evenly matched and played outdoors in the summer and at Heritage Tennis Club in the winter.

Kathy also played in a women's doubles league at Heritage. Some of the women were from Japan and played with a mild style. Kathy would call for a team huddle when some of the aggressive Americans took advantage of the Japanese payers by charging the net. Kathy's message was simple: "Hit the ball hard at the charging American, she will soon back off."

Mary Flynn joins Kathy and Gene

In 1996 my mother was 74 and suffering from heart problems. My sisters were not in a good position to invite her to live with them, so Kathy and I asked her to join our home.

We expected the worst, but it turned out very well. Both my mother and I had mellowed over the years and found we could talk about books, movies and the news. She even refrained from commenting on how we were raising David, although I am sure she had to bite her tongue once or twice.

It was also good for Dave to get to know his other grandmother. Mary was very pleased that David and his friends always stopped by her room to say "hello."

While Mary did not leave our home much, she became an active member of Saint Francis through the wonderful services of Val Franke and the Minister of Care program. Mary died in 1998.

David Flynn and Carmel Football

When David was at Saint Francis School, Kathy's office was right next door to the office of School Principal Roy Rash. I am sure there were some days that David wished that his mom's office was on a different planet.

When Dave went off to the Carmel High School in Mundelein, Illinois, he was finally outside his parent's close educational involvement. Like his father, he did much better on his own.

Dave entered the Carmel Football program in sophomore year. It was a decision that Kathy had great misgivings about; but she didn't let her view influence David.

As it turned out, the football program at Carmel and later Saint Joseph's College was a great experience for David. Even when he switched from player to equipment manager in senior year, David continued to learn about teamwork, respect and commitment that will affect the rest of his life.

Summary

Kathy and I realized how blessed we were with our life together and with the addition of David. We knew for many years that the odds of growing old together were not good. That gave us extra reasons to live the life we wanted and not march to other people's drums.

Like my father before me, I am forever grateful for Kathy joining my life and for the son that gave us so much joy.

Chapter 11:

Signs Leading to Ministry

In 1988 Dave Flynn was a 2^(nd) Grader at Montessori School and getting ready for his 1^(st) Communion at Saint Francis. Kathy signed on to teach a 3^(rd) grade Religious Education class; it was nothing special, she had done the same at HOC before and after we were married.

In 1990 Kathy began leading a 7^(th) grade religious education class. One day she bought a silly looking rubber chicken for her class. She began to throw the chicken to students that made very "insightful comments" in class. That student would then toss the chicken to the owner of the next "insightful" comment. The students began to have a lot of fun learning about God's love for them. Kathy was having fun as well.

Over a three or four month period something opened for Kathy that tied together her values, her past education and her love for working with people.

Ron Gollatz Arrives

After a short trial period, Kathy began working full time for Director of Religious Education (DRE) Bill Krueger. That same year Fr. Ron Gollatz replaced Fr. Richard Valker as pastor.

Ron gave Kathy great encouragement and support for both her Masters Degree studies and her ministry at Saint Francis. They both shared a common vision of ministry and a common sense of humor.

Perhaps the only area of serious disagreement between Kathy and Ron was dining. Ron's tastes leaned heavily toward French gourmet and Kathy's to American basic. On at least two occasions that caused for great stories:

- On one occasion Parish Council & staff were holding a "bring a main-dish" meal and meeting. Someone brought a bucket of Kentucky Fried Chicken. Ron spent most of the meeting watching for the owner the KFC bucket; sure that is was Kathy; it wasn't.

- For Ron's 50th birthday, the Arvidsons and we invited him to dinner at Le Titi de Paris. When Ron arrived at the Flynn home to pick us up, a surprise birthday party with forty people greeted him. Ron kept asking, "When are we leaving for the restaurant?"

The Signs for Ministry

Kathy wasn't looking for a serious role in ministry; it found her. And as she became more involved in the Saint Francis Religious Education program and with her studies at Loyola University, she found that the many strands of her life came together.

Chapter 12:

Loyola IPS

In 1992 Kathy started working on a Masters Degree in Pastoral Studies at the Loyola Institute for Pastoral Studies (IPS).

The combination of stimulating classes at IPS and working full time with the Saint Francis community was awesome. Her work at St. Francis gave her great material for her discussions and papers at IPS. Her ISP studies gave her ideas to share and apply at St. Francis.

IPS Environment

The IPS mission statement highlights:

- Prepare professional ministers for service in the church and in the world.

- Offer programs, curriculum, and formation to meet the needs of adult learners
    o In initial preparation for ministry
    o Those choosing to further develop their ministerial skills and competencies

Kathy found the above mission statement and reality to be in sync. The student body was quite diverse in terms of age, ministry experience and even geography. Taking classes with priests from Africa and Christian Brothers from Australia highlighted that we are part of a universal church.

Kathy had many great courses at IPS, but she probably learned the most in the following four courses:

- *Dynamics of Liturgy* by John Buscemi.
- *Gospel of Mark* by Fr. William Thompson, S.J.
- *Leadership in Ministry* by James Whitehead PhD & Evelyn Whitehead PhD.
- *Focus on Jesus* by Ann Graff, PhD.

Dynamics of Liturgy

John Buscemi's course brought great insights and many practical ideas that Kathy could apply to her ministry. John was also part of the architecture team that worked on the design of Saint Francis de Sales Church built in 1986.

Perhaps the best way to share the value of this class is to quote from a paper Kathy submitted on July 27th, 1993:

> *I decided early, to keep a reflective journal at the end of each week. I was loyal to it most of the time. In the course of doing so, I realized that one theme which I kept coming back to and which I think ran through the discussions in class was that of story telling.*
>
> *Being Irish, stories have always been a strong part of my life. I guess I never realized how much a part until this class. The reality of this hit home in the past two weeks when I was driving my son to join the rest of the family at*

the families' summer cottage. We stopped for lunch in the town we have visited for my forty-five years. He turned to me and said: "Mom, remember what your dad used to say about this place," repeating a funny line of my dad's. My son is eleven years-old, my dad has been dead for thirty years, obviously the only way he could have known what my dad said was through the telling of a story either by myself or another. For an instant though, my aunt and uncle, cousin and myself were laughing and transported in some magical way to thirty-five years ago. Suddenly my dad's presence was there. You could almost touch it.

If it were not for these past six weeks, a great deal of the significance of the preceding story would not have hit me the way it did. You see, after six weeks I bring back to my ministry and to my personal life a love for the story we as Catholics, as followers of Jesus of Nazareth, have to tell; are mandated to tell. I want to tell the stories so that Jesus' presence is there in the same way my dad was.

The way we tell the story is so critical.

And later in the same paper:

I will no longer see planning a liturgy as something which has a lot in common with the answering of a parish phone to hear someone say, "Hey, how much does a mass cost? I wanna buy a mass."

I will no longer get an adrenalin rush two minutes before the celebration of first Eucharist running around to be sure the banner carriers know when to start up the aisle. I hope I will have made families feel welcome; I will try to make the telling of the story and the sharing of the meaning with these young people an event that speaks to the "bones" of those who join us, those who are members of our faith community.

Student and Study Buddies

Kathy was an excellent student and took an active part in class discussions.

Most of her courses also required writing three or four papers. Kathy had a natural talent for writing: she could get to the important message in a way that read well and connected with her life. Only occasionally did her papers have spelling or punctuation errors; those were sure signs that she was very tired.

Even beyond class and papers, however, Kathy benefited by finding a wonderful set of "study buddies." Kathy, Jackie Froehlich, and Mary Beth Frystack took many of their classes together. They supported each other in difficult classes with laughter and serious discussions. They also learned from each other's experiences. Jackie Froehlich would later recall:

In the classroom, Kathy always surfaced as a leader. Other students were impressed by her gifts, her practicality and her sense of humor.

Kathy was always able to translate our course work into very practical, useable, pastoral terms. It was clear that she intended to use every bit of her IPS education and experiences in service to her ministry. She approached each class with that in mind and because of it, her fellow classmates benefited as well.

The Gospel of Mark

Jackie also recalled the scripture course she took with Kathy:

Kathy really enjoyed our scripture course with Father Thompson, S.J. He enjoyed a wonderful reputation as a scripture scholar and we both looked forward to taking this class. Father Thompson identified the Gospel of Mark as a gospel for those who were suffering. During the course of this class, Father Thompson was diagnosed with cancer. We, students, witnessed his suffering first hand and his reflections in class took on a whole new dimension. Everyone who took that class was changed by it. Kathy and I had many discussions about the real message of the Gospel of Mark. Kathy knew so much and shared so much about the experience of coping with cancer, not only with me but also with the class as we would gather week after week after Father Thompson's diagnosis, wondering whether or not he was well enough to teach that week or if we would have a substitute instructor. Kathy brought a special understanding and compassion to that situation and our fellow classmates appreciated her sharing and respected her for her openness. It was an invaluable learning experience for all of us, especially for me.

Author Henri Nouwen

ISP studies brought Kathy into contact with a great faculty. It also brought her into contact with the writings of Dutch priest Henri J.M. Nouwen. Kathy read at least eight of his books and always had one at her bedside table and beside her exercise bike. It was the treat for the most boring part of her workout.

Her favorite Nouwen book was *The Return of The Prodigal Son – A Story of Homecoming*[25]. She even had a 45-inch poster of the Rembrandt painting of the same name.

Darkness and Light

Looking at Kathy's copy of *The Return of the Prodigal Son* shows comments on most pages, but the message on Darkness in chapter nine seems most appropriate:

"People who have come to know the joy of God do not deny the darkness, but they choose not to live in it. They claim that the light that shines in the darkness can be

---

[25] An Image Book, published by Doubleday, New York, New York © 1992

trusted more than the darkness itself and that a little bit of light can dispel a lot of darkness."

Harry Lane, John Lane, and Kathy all believed in the presence of darkness and evil. Harry studied it in the seminary, John saw it on the streets in his police work and Kathy had seen the victims of evil. Including:

- A Nazi concentration camp survivor who felt guilty that she was the only family member to survive.
- Adults suffering from terrible childhood sexual abuse from parents and other adults.
- Wives battered by abusive husbands.

Kathy's faith and believe in the "light of God" allowed her to move beyond the evil that she could not change, but it was not always easy.

Kathy knew that we are all God's children and like the prodigal son, we all need a homecoming to our loving Father. She had a growing sense that her return to the father would be a welcoming one. She tried to show the same compassion to those she worked with.

Chapter 13:

Kathy as DRE

Saint Francis Religious Education

In July 1992 Kathy began working as Assistant to DRE & Deacon Bill Krueger. She had a tiny office that was once a storage room. She loved it because it had a big window that opened to cool the office. For some reason, the main work area of the School/RE office was usually 90 degrees, all year round.

Let me begin by saying that working in the same office with Carol Mantone and Rosie McGrath was priceless. Rosie was the lead secretary for the School and Carol for the RE office. Rosie and Carol found ways for all the office staff to work together despite many demands of a school with 600 students and a Religious Education program with 1,200 students. Kathy valued their warmth, laughter and support the rest of her life.

Junior High Impact

Kathy's first assignment was coordinating the junior-high Religious Education program. Bill expected Kathy to follow his normal formula:

Find 25 adults willing to teach 28 Monday night sessions.

Kathy and Pastoral Associate George Koll put their heads together and came up with a whole new approach, giving the junior-high students the option to choose from 25 different offerings, including:

- Six different 4-week courses worth 4 points each
- Service projects worth 2 points each
- One-day retreats worth 2 points each
- Prayer opportunities worth 1 point

The students could make any choices, as long as they achieved the required number of points. Once Kathy and George worked out the kinks, the approach had many benefits, including:

- People who might shy away from a 28-week commitment were willing to sign-up to lead a 4-week mini course.
- Catechists could lead a 4-week course, take a break and then lead the same course to a different set of kids.
- The mini-courses had titles like "Who Are Our Heroes" and "Dealing with Tough Times" that might attract sixth and seventh grade students. The material did a great job at connecting the kids with Christ's love and message.
- The process got junior high kids and their parents talking sometimes about different options.

I helped teach two of the mini-courses, but my lead assignment from Kathy was the annual Paint-a-house service project.

We took fourteen junior high kids and fourteen parents and painted the outside of a house in one day. We started the day with a reminder that Christians are called to help the needy and not just to write checks to pay for others to help. By the end of the day the kids and parents were covered with paint, but also had a sense that they had really helped someone. We ended with a prayer and a "thank you" to the elderly couple that trusted us with their home.

Course: Leadership in Ministry: Power & Authority

During the summer of 1993 Kathy was taking a four-week IPS course on Leadership in Ministry taught by James Whitehead PhD & Evelyn Whitehead PhD. This course was very timely because her working relationship with Bill Kruger had broken down.

Kathy and Bill had worked well together as long as Bill was "boss." Things started to get ugly when the pastor decided Kathy and Bill would be co-directors, with both reporting to him.

The Whitehead course helped Kathy understand that Saint Francis and indeed many Catholic parishes are dealing with conflicts between "Clericalism" and "empowerment". The Whiteheads pointed out that while some deacons and lay Pastoral Associates complained of being treated as 2nd class citizens by the Church, they were very comfortable amassing power and treating volunteers as 3rd class citizens.

The Whiteheads saw the need for broad parish empowerment. In their book *Promise of Partnership* they state: "Effective leaders, like successful parents, learn the demanding discipline of letting go. Empowering those in their care, genuine leaders nurture others toward maturity and finally welcome them as peers."

The course helped Kathy understand that some parish leaders are comfortable only when they can operate on a basis of authority or paternalism. The course also helped her understand her leadership goals and how they are intertwined with life-goals. In a July 19, 1993 reflection paper Kathy writes:

> *The second mistake I made was in thinking he and I were looking at our ministries in terms of stewardship and collaboration. I admit this is not always something I do, but I sincerely believe this is the direction I am trying to move.*
>
> *In my personal life, when my son was one year old I developed cancer. My husband and I thought we had been blessed with everything we had ever wanted. We had had problems conceiving and when he was born on Christmas day we felt truly blessed.*
>
> *A year later at the onset, and in the reoccurrence of the disease, we both have come to realize our son is just a part of that great scheme we call our lives where we are stewards, servants, not owners. Our greatest service to our son is to empower him in a way where we can let go. Whenever that time of letting go is, pray he will have the maturity to go on and keep the message of Jesus of Nazareth alive in his life.*
>
> *I have pledged myself; I will do the same in my ministry: I will never take*

ownership of a program. I look to the staff, which we have in our parish, and to the resources we have in our community of believers to serve the needs of the body of Christ. And I see an abundance of rich stewards. Collaboration is a must.

Kathy as Director of Religious Education

The following year Bill Krueger moved to a new role, managing parish maintenance, and Kathy became sole DRE. During this year and the next she used her people skills and her IPS training to energize almost all parts of the program.

By this point the K-5 grade portion of the program had grown far beyond the ability to support 800 kids on Saturday morning. In addition, more and more kids were in sports that conflicted with Saturday studies. Kathy solved this by adding after-school sessions on two weekdays.

The added days and Kathy's continued sanity was supported by a group of dedicated people willing to step forward and sign up to coordinate specific sessions. Others signed on to be leaders for specific grades. A year or two later another set of parents signed on to hold office on a Religious Education Advisory Board. Not only did they join the board, they took it seriously.

As more of the day-to-day effort went to the session coordinators and grade leaders, Kathy could focus on recruitment, training and spiritual development for the volunteers. Many parents said they wanted to help but felt they were totally unqualified to be a catechist. Much as she did once with parents of children with heart defects, she convinced most hesitant parents that they could be great catechists and that she and the team leaders would help them.

Kathy remained very accessible to all the team leaders, catechists and even the volunteer high school students.

First Communion

Each year about 300 second graders receive their First Communion at Saint Francis. This was a major effort that began with parent meetings in September and concluded in May of each year. Kathy, Carol Mantone, Maria Joyce, the 2nd grade school teachers and 2nd grade Religious Education catechists all played an extensive role.

Nancy Buschman led the effort for several years with great skill as 2nd Grade lead Catechist. One day she quietly told Kathy that she had to leave this volunteer post because her family was moving to a different part of the Chicago area. Fortunately Karen Nolen stepped forward, even when she already knew how much work was involved.

Public Speaking

Kathy hated to talk in front of groups of people. Her knees would shake and her hands tremble. But her voice did not betray her anxiety and her words carried a message of God's love for us, and the need to empower each other.

In many ways, Kathy applied what she wrote about during that sleepless night in 1975:

Communication is certainly lacking in many today. Just the ability to express ourselves in words has begun to suffer in today's society. Those who deal with the public should always speak plainly. Lincoln was a master of simple words.

Guilt-Free Service

Across all religions there is often a shortage of volunteers for specific roles. Those that do volunteer are often thanked repeatedly for their efforts. However, should volunteers indicate they cannot renew their effort for the next year; leaders often try to force reconsideration. A leader might say: "If you quit, we will have to turn away 30 kids from the program."

Kathy thought such leader behavior was plain wrong. People should be thanked for what they do and not harassed that they can't do more. She understood that people need breaks or even need to do something entirely different.

Kathy cared about the volunteers themselves and not just what they could do for her program. Most of the volunteers felt this care and tried to pass it on to others they worked with.

Saint Francis School

Kathy saw working with Saint Francis School as part of her ministry. She worked actively with Principle Roy Rash and all the teachers.

One of the main ways she touched the school was the weekly school Mass. Each homeroom was responsible for two Masses in the course of the year. Each week Kathy worked with a teacher and five students planning the next Mass.

Kathy also worked with the eight grade teachers to plan the graduation service. While she sometimes played hard-to-get in this role, she loved doing it. Planning with ten of the graduates took place over a five or six week period. Kathy made sure the student planning team was comprised of a cross-section of the students and not just "A" students.

Children's Catechumenate

Ron asked Kathy to start up a catechumen program for children that were out of the normal flow of sacraments. While the Archdiocese had a great program guide, running such a program took a lot of time and effort. Fortunately for Kathy, Beth Husted and Rita Wojanowski answered a request for help.

While Beth and Rita lead most of the sessions for the children, Kathy worked closely with the parents.

Most of the parents were a delight to work with. The exceptions were situations where one or both parents were treating the program as an extension of a divorce court custody battle. Kathy had great respect for several dads who came to support their children even when a mother was sending a message: "Reject your dad and his religion."

Parents have so much good to give their children; it pained Kathy to see the occasional parent who chose to give mistrust and prejudice.

Certification

Kathy's formation and studies at Loyola helped prepare her for her parish ministry role. Concurrent with her studies she began the process for DRE certification by the Archdiocese of Chicago Office of Religious Education. This process was quite extensive, involving letters of recommendations, lengthy questionnaires and a 2-hour review by a formal committee. Kathy was granted the DRE certification in 1995 and was later granted certification as a Pastorate Associate of the Office of Ministry. Cardinal George gave Kathy the formal document at a meeting of Pastoral Associates in March 2001.

Ireland and Things Irish

Kathy's job was very hectic for ten months of the year. However, June/July was quite calm and gave Kathy a chance to enjoy the warm weather and think about the new school year.

In July 1998 we went to Ireland for a week. I had three days of business meetings, which gave Kathy time to wonder around Dublin and see the sites. She even acquired a taste for Guinness beer.

One day we took a nine-county bus tour through southeast Ireland. We left the bus for lunch on a riverboat and for stops at the Waterford Crystal factory and several historic sights. Most of the day was spent speeding along rural roads while the driver/tour guide pointed out interesting sites of past battles or castle ruins. In one town we passed a large statute of Fr. Flynn, a local priest who lead an unsuccessful revolt against the British.

Travelers to Ireland will each have their own set of stories, but a common theme seems to be the sincere friendliness of the people and the realization that this small island suffered terribly under British rule and still kept their sense of humor and joy of life.

Chapter 14:

Parish Ministry

Some of Kathy's friends from IPS worked in parishes where the staff came together once a month for a one-hour meeting. That was not the case at St. Francis.

Pastor Ron Gollatz fostered extensive joint discussions within the parish staff and between staff and parish council. This made for weekly 3-hour staff meetings plus other joint meetings during the course of the month.

This level of joint communication highlights the fact that parish ministry involves much more than "working your assigned area;" it is ministering to the parish as a whole.

New Staff Role

Kathy left the DRE role in July 1999. Her new assignments focused on working with engaged couples, planning weddings, supporting the marriage annulment process and even leading communion services at Lexington Nursing home.

Wedding Preparations

One of Kathy's new responsibilities was working with couples to arrange their marriage. In the Catholic Church this involves collecting forms, taking some depositions, and coordinating the wedding rehearsal as well as the actual wedding ceremony.

Fr. Ron and Fr. Jim were responsible for the wedding they presided at; Kathy was responsible for the weddings where visiting priests were presiding. There were quite a few weddings that fell into the latter category because the bride & groom might ask a priest formerly assigned to St. Francis, a priest relative, or even a college chaplain to preside.

A number of the engaged couples were already living and working in distant cities and had limited face-to-face time with Kathy. Despite many potential problems, everything seemed to work out in the end. Wherever possible, Kathy tried to give the mother of the groom her three suggested rules:

- Show up
- Shut-up
- Dress in beige

Annulments

Kathy also worked with individuals seeking marriage annulments. Her role was to assist individuals in understanding the annulment process and in submitting the proper material to the Archdiocese Marriage Tribunal. The notice she put in the parish bulletin portrays how she approached this assignment:

A TIME FOR HEALING

There are few things in life that can be as traumatic or as hurtful to an individual or family as is the breakup of a marriage. Often times this is made even worse by the belief that the Church closes the door to the parties involved. This is as painful as anything one can think they will ever feel.

Just as Christ would never close the door on anyone who turns to him, so too must we be as open and willing to minister to those who suffer from such hurt. Divorce and annulment are surrounded with rumors and misconceptions that should be put to rest.

St. Francis now wants to reach out to those who suffer. We want to be a part of the solution, not the problem. We are starting a support ministry and there are brochures on the bookstand in the Gathering Space of the Church. Kathy Flynn, our Pastoral Associate, will help you find the answers you are looking for from the Church. If you are overwhelmed by the ideas of having to fill our extensive forms, Kathy will help you, and we will walk with you through the process.

Everything will be strictly **confidential**. Fill out the brochure or call Kathy at the parish office.

Turn this time of turmoil into a time of healing and peace. (St. Francis Parish Bulletin, 8/26/01 and following weeks)

Lay Deaconate

Another new role for Kathy was supervision of our parish couple in the Lay Deaconate program, Sue and Bob Arvidson. We were already friends with the Arvidsons, going back to David Flynn inviting 4th grade classmate Tim Arvidson to our home after school.

Kathy fulfilled the supervisory function largely by planning joint dinners for the four of us.

We would spend two hours over good food and talk at Giodano's restaurant. The dinners gave Bob and Sue a chance to talk about what they were studying in the program and how it might apply to the future deaconate role. Equally important, the dinner gave both couples a chance to unwind with close friends.

Kathy and I had great respect for the many Deaconate Program couples that spent four years of evening effort in addition to raising families and day jobs.

Kathy and I were very proud to attend Bob's ordination to the deaconate in May 2001.

God's Refuge

Moving from the DRE role was a mixed blessing for Kathy. It gave her great flexibility to work when she felt good and to rest when she was tired or ill, as she increasingly was. On the other hand, she missed the constant interaction with the kids, the catechists, and the leaders.

Kathy found comfort in reading Morning and Evening Prayer[26]. Between the prayers and

---

[26] From ancient times the Church has had the custom of celebrating each day with common prayers. The custom soon grew of assigning special times to common prayer, for example, the last hour of the day, when evening draws on and the lamp is lighted; or the first hour, when night draws to a close with the rising of the sun. The Second Vatican Council saw the important of renewing the Liturgy of the Hours and making it more accessible. (From Christian Prayer: The Liturgy of the Hours, Catholic Book Publishing Co., NYC, 1979)

meditation, she spent about 45-minutes in the morning and 30 minutes in the evening.

As a couple, we began to read Night Prayer together. This ten-minute prayer had great meaning for us. One of my favorite passages occurs on Sunday night:

> ANT: Night holds no terrors for me sleeping under God's wings.

> He who dwells in the shelter of the Most High and abides in the shade of the Almighty says to the Lord: "My refuge, my stronghold, my God in whom I trust!"
> It is he who will free you from the snare of the fowler who seeks to destroy you; he will conceal you with his pinions and under his wings you will find refuge.

Kathy did seek God's refuge. It gave her the strength to live in the shadow of her many illnesses. It also gave her the strength to carry on after Judy Curtin was diagnosed with Leukemia in August 1999 and died in January 2000.

Judy's death was very hard on Kathy. Kathy's faith and working with the people at Saint Francis helped, over time, soften her grief.

Conclusion

Some political leaders speak with regret that they did not serve during times of great crisis to demonstrate their many strengths.

Kathy's life journey shows that we can all be touched and touch the lives of others. Kathy touched many lives, but she always felt blessed by the people she worked with and ministered to.

Kathy was always mindful of her roots, those who came before us and helped us become the people we are. She was also fortunate that her family and friends challenged her to look for signs along her life journey and to venture into new territories.

Chapter 15:

Ideas for the Journey

I initially called this chapter "lessons from Kathy's journey." Then I realized that Kathy would take exception to the words "lesson" or "rules" because it implies what other people should learn from her life.

She would be much more comfortable with the statement that these are ideas she learned from parents and friends, or even by trial and error along the way. And, if other people want to think about them and use a few, that's OK with her.

#1: Life is a journey; and the journey you begin may not be the one you end[27]

- Some people believe that life begins at some future point when you finish school or get married. Kathy lived life to the fullest at every stage of her life.
- Kathy believed and taught me to enjoy the fruits of work and not always be saving for some future point. She saw her mom and dad enjoy life.
- Don't panic if you don't know what you will do when you grow-up. Kathy found her perfect role at age 43.

---

[27] I would like to thank Michelle Titterton for sharing the lessons she learned from J.R.R. Token's *The Hobbit* while studying at the University of Notre Dame. I used her lessons to verbalize points 1-3 above.

#2: There are signs along the journey, but you must look for them.

- Kathy was not looking for a new relationship when she met Gene, quite the contrary. But she saw the signs of shared values, and looked deeper.
- She was not looking for a lay ministry vocation, but a modest catechist stint opened something that brought many of the pieces of her life together. The Holy Spirit can touch us all if we look.

#3: People will help you along your journey.

- As a pre-teen, teen and young adult Kathy had great help from dedicated teachers, friends, coworkers and neighbors. Sometimes small acts of kindness make a big difference in the lives of young people. Often just listening is a big help.
- You can find new friends throughout your life. When she was forty years old, Kathy thought she had found all the close friends she would ever have. How wrong she was; moving to the Saint Francis community opened the door to many additional close friends.
- Kathy found wonderful support for the Saint Francis Religious Education program. Each year, hundreds of wonderful adults and teens took part as coordinators, team leaders,

catechists, secretaries and service volunteers. Other wonderful people helped her form a Religious Education Board and a Children Catechumenate program.

- Kathy was not a pillar of strength, in fact none of us are. We were very fortunate to find each other and to work well together in caring for each other and in making a good marriage.

#4: Children can learn so much from their parents.

- Give your children "roots" and "wings." Sharing your core values will help give your children roots. The harder part is letting your children take wings by making choices, some of which can lead to setbacks and bruises. Too often well-meaning parents, like Mary Flynn, try to 'steer' their children to safe decisions and careers. Kathy saw the wisdom of letting young adults make their own decisions.

- It takes time and interactive talk for parents to share core values. Kathy had this on the trips to Florida and while her father was recovering from his heart attacks.

- It's OK for kids to see that you are not perfect; they will love you anyway.

#5: Prayer and Medication are richly rewarding

- Kathy started morning and evening prayer because it was a directive for Pastoral Associates. She then found it to be very rewarding.
- There is much in life, and in the Church, that is unfair, confusing and conflicting. By taping the "Serenity Prayer" to her make-up mirror, Kathy repeated the words:

> God grant me the serenity to accept the things I cannot change, courage to change the things I can and wisdom to know the difference.

#6: If you have serious illnesses, find doctors that treat body and spirit.

- Kathy had a great medical team lead by Frank Murphy M.D. for 35 years and by Walt Bajgrowicz, M.D. for 20 years. They, along with Oncologist Leon Dragon, M.D. and GI Wanchai Sangchantr, M.D., helped her lead an active life and not an illness-focused life.
- When Kathy and I were newly engaged I called Dr. Murphy to talk about Kathy. When he called back that evening (amazing in itself) I asked if Kathy shouldn't follow his directives more

closely and take life more slowly. He replied, "No, it's better that she push the boundaries and live life to her fullest potential. Her body would tell her when she was going too far."

#7: Treat People with respect

- At Kathy's wake many people told me how she always took the time to stop and say a kind word. It did not matter if these were kids in school or senior citizens.
- When Kathy's office was at the School/Religious Education building, her door was always open for kids to stop in and say hello. With Gumby toys and a little candy, there was always something to talk about.

#8: Share the Good News of Christ, but don't be judgmental and don't pretend you have all the answers.

- Accept people as they are. Some teens might come to help only because they wanted to build a better college application. That's fine; the Holy Spirit works in wonderful ways.
- True parish leadership is about empowering others to share in Christ's work; it is not about power and authority.

#9: When all else fails, your dog will still be at your side.

- From the first dog given by uncle John Lane when she was ten, to the puppy we got when David went off to college, dogs have been an important part of Kathy's life.
- Kathy got great satisfaction and strength from her work at Saint Francis, but some days were totally frustrating. Her dog, and sometimes son and husband, gave her the support to regroup.
- When necessary, Kathy and the dogs could watch an entire X-Files season (24 chapters) over a weekend. The trials of agents Mulder and Scully were somehow very relaxing. And to quote Agent Mulder: "I have been on the bridge that spans two worlds...."
- Spouses travel, children have lives of their own, but dogs live for their owners. They are a true gift from God and deserve to be called "man's best friend."

The End